EATING OUT
IN EDINBURGH AND GLASGOW

the SCOTLAND *on* SUNDAY *guide to*
EATING OUT
IN EDINBURGH AND GLASGOW

JOANNA BLYTHMAN

illustrated by Rosamund Fowler

CANONGATE

First Published in 1990 by
Canongate Publishing Ltd
16 Frederick Street
Edinburgh

British Library Cataloguing in Publication Data
available on request

ISBN 0-86241-308-7

Typeset by Hewer Text, Edinburgh.
Printed and bound by Cox & Wyman Ltd, Reading.

CONTENTS

FOREWORD

I first met Joanna Blythman in her good food shop called Fraiche just round the corner from Haymarket station in Edinburgh.

I knew what an uncompromising palate she had just by looking round the shelves. No junk, no rubbish. Everything had class from the organic vegetables to the summer truffles, chanterelles, water asparagus and salads. Fraiche was famous for its real cheeses, picked for their unpasteurised taste and flavour and most of them handmade in Scotland. The Blythman philosophy was to place traditional local produce in its rightful context and to encourage the new things that were happening on the food front.

Eventually Fraiche went bust. It was ahead of its time. A large part of the business came from young chefs who were looking for high quality raw materials and so when Joanna Blythman was made the first food and cookery editor of *Scotland on Sunday* she already had firm links with the good food movement in Scottish restaurants. These were strengthened by the paper's Eating Out column which has established itself as a highly objective and idiosyncratic guide.

A quarter of a century ago it would have been an uphill job to compile as exciting a guide as this to eating out in the two great cities of the Central Belt. In Glasgow there was the Malmaison where captains of industry lunched off *volaille Jean Bart* and other manifestations of classical *haute cuisine*. Rogano's in those days was having to import its oysters from Cornwall and the pick of the rest was a Peter Evans eating house with decor by David Hicks.

In Edinburgh the Pompadour room was serving lobster cocktail for 14/6 and at the North British hotel a pianist played selections from 'Lilac Time' in the Grill Room while the waiters wheeled in *terrine maison* and *crevettes Marie Rose*. It was, as Americans say, something other.

The revolution that has overtaken eating out in urban Scotland is chronicled in the entries that follow. The advent of the new wave Indian restaurants, wine bars with drinkable vintages, atmospheric cafes, wholefood oases, even workers' co-operatives make heady reading.

All culinary life is here from the People's Palace with its worthy beansprouts and healthgiving herbal teas to the frankly erotic not to say licentious gastronomic bordello of Byres Road which features 'a windowful of good-looking tarts'. Not the sort of thing

7

that would go down in Edinburgh at all.

This is an essential handbook for Festival and Burrell visitors and a spirited year-round guide for citizens who care about real food.

Derek Cooper

PREFACE

Most eating-out guides fall into two camps. The first (and most easily discarded) are those sponsored by promotional bodies who would like to exploit the eating-out market as a way of pushing their product. Some are more impressive than others, but irrespective of whether they are advocating say, Scotland as a centre for tourism, or the business ventures of a self-appointed local restaurateurs association, you can trust what they say about as much as a random search through the Yellow Pages.

Then there are those guides which although they may receive backing from a commercial concern, (*The Good Food Guide* is the noble exception to this rule), genuinely try to report in an objective and rigorous manner. Some rely on consumer reports, others, on the guidance of local inspectors. By and large, one can set some store by their recommendations.

The trouble with Scotland, however, is that otherwise commendable guides see it as a region. London-based guides recognise that in the interests of good geographical coverage, Scottish establishments must be included. But as the focus of interest spreads northwards, so the conviction of the guides, and their reporters, diminishes. The cracks show, not so much in coverage of outlying or remote areas, because these tend to fit with romantic southern notions of Scotland as a land of misty glens and noble stags, but when it comes to reporting on Scotland's urban areas. Ask inhabitants of, or visitors to, Scotland's two major cities – Edinburgh and Glasgow – whether there is any independent guide which gives them substantial critical coverage of the multitude of eating-out possibilities (such as London's *Time Out Guide*), and the answer, until now, would have been a resounding no.

This book is designed to change all that. It is an independent review of the best eating-out possibilities in the two cities, which offers in-depth insights into its subject matter. It is not about promoting the cause of tourism, by trying to convince you that Edinburgh and Glasgow are international pinnacles of perfection for fine food. In this sense, although Edinburgh and Glasgow are its remits, it is not a parochial book. It is, however, a book which feels at home with its subject matter. As such, I hope that it puts its finger on the pulse and describes how well certain establishments operate, given availability of disposable income, access to good raw materials and the other elements that go together to stimulate a healthy restaurant culture. Each restaurant included in this book has been visited by me personally in early 1990, some on more than one occasion. All visits were anonymous and the meals paid for by *Scotland on Sunday*, as a fortuitous spin-off of its weekly restaurant review section. Each profile reflects my own opinions and preoccupations. You may or may not share them, but I think they are sufficiently up-front to allow each reader to draw his or her own conclusions. I have incorporated the wealth of informal and formal information which came my way, concerning restaurants, into each write-up. But the reviews are, in the end, the product of my personal impressions, not an artificial consensus of disparate views.

To make this guide simpler to use restaurants are rated as follows:

♟ 1 chef's hat – good food

♟♟ 2 chef's hats – very good food

♟♟♟ 3 chef's hats – excellent food

This rating evaluates the cooking skills of the establishment, not comfort, atmosphere or any other issue.

The restaurants which are included in this guide offer, in my opinion, honest food which comes over in execution as it has been described on the menu, and eschews unnecessary pretension. Some of them are excellent even in international terms, others are simply decent performers within limited boundaries. Certain ground rules have been applied. First, that they actually produce real food, cooked on the spot, rather than relying on the burgeoning product list of ready-prepared foods from catering suppliers. Second, that they use fresh, locally obtained ingredients as much as possible. All of them are worthy of your business.

JOANNA BLYTHMAN August 1990

INTRODUCTION

In as much as anyone can claim to have no axe to grind in the Which Is Best? – Edinburgh or Glasgow debate, I think that I can. I have spent exactly half my life in each city and have, therefore, a foot in both camps. Commentators sometimes assert that too much is made of the difference between the two, and in general, they may have a point. But when it comes to food, there is no doubt in my mind that they are two very different worlds.

Edinburgh

Edinburgh is an introverted, class-ridden city which rewards conformity and tradition in its restaurants. Simply stated, Glaswegians like to spend it, Edinburgh people like to hoard it. While Glaswegians enjoy spending money on fripperies like eating out, well-heeled Edinburgh residents spend it on school fees, even if that means eating beans on toast for tea. Change and innovation is viewed with suspicion, and pedigree counts. Flash new restaurants with post-modern decor cut no ice in Edinburgh until someone you trust gives it a reference based on repeat visits. Quintessential Edinburgh eating establishments like the Lower Aisle and the Laigh, sum up the qualities that real Edinburgh-types like : historic or old world settings, unostentatious surroundings which betray quiet good taste, simply cooked, traditional food without frills.

Restaurateurs face a daunting prospect in Edinburgh. First they have to figure out how to price their menus at a level which can sustain them, but still attract the tight-pursed punters. Second, they have to show caution before introducing any untried or untested restaurant concept lest it wither and die.

What this spawns, is a hard core of restaurants operating from unspectacular if pleasant environments which offer little in the way of excitement or change, but much in terms of good value and reliability.

Glasgow

Glaswegians love style, not least in their eating environment. They are open to new concepts in food and dining and generally happy to try new things. Glasgow is also a bigger city, (which is reflected in the much wider range of good middle-range eating places within the city centre), and its population is much more genuinely cosmopolitan. Glaswegians of all social classes feel happier about spending their disposable income. This is altogether an encouraging climate for restaurateurs: more prospective customers around and easier to draw them in.

Extroversion shows through at all levels. Glasgow has made a conspicuous success of the bustling, urban brasserie, as examples like the Triangle, the Penguin Cafe and Cafe Gandolfi testify – a category of eating which goes down like a damp squib in Edinburgh. Eclectic menus, which draw on influences from all over the world with no one cultural identity, have stood the test of time here and worked.

But, style without content is the current Glasgow food disease. It is seen at its most acute in areas of the city which are said to be undergoing regeneration. Here you'll find the flashed up buildings which are the product of the property developers dream. It has been deemed that they shall have restaurants, but the small matter of food seems to have benefited from about as much creative thought as the pot plants, and probably from the same person.

This malaise is not restricted to areas being upgraded. In the established centre itself, you can find a number of design-conscious establishments which, if they were in London, would be serving food which went some way to matching the style. In Glasgow, the disparity may be tangible.

Scottish Food

In all but a handful of time-warped restaurants, the Edinburgh-Glasgow restaurant scene has abandoned the worst clichés attached to Scottish food. The days of escalope Marie-Stuart and beef Balmoral are receding into the Celtic twilight where they deserve to remain. In urban Scotland, where restaurants serve the indigenous population first and foremost, and tourism second, no one much ever believed in them anyway.

This doesn't mean that our food has been internationalised, simply that restaurants are redefining what 'Scots' food might be. This identity expresses itself in terms of ingredients, not cooking method. For years, the old mythology that Scotland had the world's 'finest natural larder' was put about, which may have boosted the sales of Scottish produce abroad, but did nothing for the home market who saw absolutely no evidence of it in day-to-day reality.

Slowly but surely – progress, refrigerated transport, consumer demand, however you like to explain it – more prime Scottish foodstuffs are finding their way into good restaurants. Curiously, at a time when retail customers are struggling to track down anything other than the more prosaic types of fresh fish and shellfish in the shops that serve them, the choice of prime fish in peak condition on offer to restaurants in Scotland has never been greater. This situation is mirrored with artisan Scottish farmhouse cheeses. You'll be lucky to track them down in your local delicatessen or supermarket, but any restaurant worth its salt should be able to offer you a decent selection. The same applies to the less run-of-the-mill varieties of fresh vegetables and herbs – restaurants have ready access to them while the consumer at home has problems – which gives regular diners-out a definite advantage, (and lazy restaurateurs fewer and fewer excuses).

More and more, you may come across restaurants which offer say, a half dozen oysters, a plate of smoked venison or salmon and a cheese board of ripe, handmade cheese. They may not present themselves as Scottish restaurants, or wish to be associated with the tackiness of the tartan food school, but they are offering an honest taste of Scotland.

An International Selection
What then, are the dominant styles in the Edinburgh-Glasgow eating scene? 'Modern' food – a blend of good local ingredients used innovatively with eclectic influences – forms the dominant style of much of the most promising, non-ethnic food to be had. Restaurants like Martin's in Edinburgh, which will blend local brill say, with Japanese style sea vegetables represent this style at its best and most opulent. In a more casual vein, eating places like the Doric Tavern and Cellar Number One in Edinburgh show what can be achieved when a bit of lateral thinking is applied to the much-abused wine bar concept.

French food, with the exception of the accomplished and well-understood nouvelle cuisine of L'Auberge in Edinburgh, or the rare glimpse of home cooking offered by La Cuisine D'Odile, the cafe in Edinburgh's French Institute, has largely been eclipsed by 'modern' cooking. The interface between the two can yield stimulating results if Edinburgh's Pierre Victoire is anything to go by. The modern movement has its limitations. There needs to be someone in the kitchen who has good taste – a safeguard you cannot take for granted. One restaurant excluded from this book served a salad of marvellous scallops, topped with a collection of ephemera which included a cape gooseberry, a slice of star fruit, miscellaneous herbs, a cherry tomato and the token Spanish strawberry. This is the sort of experience that leaves you feeling that there are nursery school tots on the loose in the kitchen.

One dull and unimaginative hallmark of much of the cooking in this 'modern' vein is its treatment of vegetables, inevitably a boring little side plate of baby corn, mangetout, boiled potatoes, carrots or courgette. This is a convention which stems from 'you need to eat your greens' type of thinking. It really is time that it was abandoned and some creative thinking was given either to incorporating vegetables into the main dish, or serving one judiciously chosen specimen, interestingly cooked, designed to complement the whole.

As a general rule, with a few notable exceptions such as La Parmigiana in Glasgow or Tinelli's and Duncan's Land in Edinburgh, Italian food has not moved on from the standard trattoria mould. La Vera Cucina Italiana has still to make an impact on the manic pepper-grinding, candle-in-the-Chianti-bottle school. Perhaps there is little incentive for it to do so, since in Edinburgh and Glasgow, as elsewhere, the standard trattoria formula continues to be a popular, and one imagines profitable, one. Within the standard conventions of Scottish-Italian food, there are some accomplished performers offering straightforward, wholesome and in the main, good value food, such as Bar Roma in Edinburgh. But they stand to be immeasurably improved with the importation of a dose of authenticity. And since pasta and pizza have been hi-jacked by the rest of the world, the competition is getting stiffer all the time. Arguably, Glasgow's finest pizza is to be had at Sannino's where Reo Stakis bought the concept from an Italian gent by the same name. Time for the Italian community to start fighting back with extra virgin olive oil, fresh basil and lashings of Parmigiano-Reggiano.

Some of the finest Indian food you'll ever eat in Britain is to be had in Edinburgh. Credit for this must go to Moussa Jogee and Dik Metha who pioneered no-compromise, Indian food through the vehicles of the Shamiana and Kalpna restaurants. Scots, pre-Shamiana and Kalpna, expected Indian food to be cheap, filling and unchallenging. They liked the flavours to be strong to penetrate post-pub alcohol soaked palates. They wanted jugs of beer and extra portions of chips. Pragmatic representatives of that community gave it to them, hence the restaurant run purely as a commercial concern with a tacit recognition amongst those involved that this was a way to make money and keep the punters happy. The fact that the food on offer bore little resemblance to what was served at home either in Scotland or in India was neither here nor there. Much the same can be said of Scottish-Chinese food (and indeed ethnic food in Britain in general) where the standing joke is that the restaurateurs prefer to cook separately for themselves and their staff.

Successful models which set benchmarks for authenticity like the Shamiana and Kalpna, offer an incentive to others to match their standards. So even the most humdrum Indian food in Edinburgh has a lot going for it. In Glasgow, the vestiges of the old 'International Gravy' live on in some of its restaurants, where the emphasis is all too often on one-dimensional flavours and massive portions.

By comparison with Chinese food in other parts of Britain, Scotland hasn't had much of a track record. Until very recently, if you had put our Chinese restaurants in the dock for a Gang of Four style trial, you would have found them guilty of several heinous crimes: mugging the mouth with blockbuster sauces, overdosing on white powder (monosodium glutamate), a liberal hand with artificial food colourings, using frozen not fresh fish. Verdict? Guilty on all counts. Encouragingly, there are signs that this is changing. More restaurants like Gourmet House in Glasgow and Loon Fung in Edinburgh are making a feature of deliciously cooked fresh fish. Corrosive sweet and sour sauces continue to be served in the cities' Chinese emporia, but discerning scrutiny of the menu can locate dishes with integrity, such as the magnificent potsticker dumplings in Glasgow's Peking Inn. A Sunday lunchtime visit to a restaurant like the Bamboo Garden in Edinburgh for a selection of Dim Sum, offers an insight into how the Chinese themselves like to eat. And there are marvels. Walk past Szechuan House in Edinburgh and it looks like a standard neighbourhood takeaway. This makes it all the more exciting when you find that it serves awe-inspiring dishes like tea-smoked duck which stay close to their Szechuan roots – and at bargain basement prices.

Lonely representatives of less familiar cuisines are making an appearance. Mata Hari, which serves Malaysian home cooking, Mai Thai offering self-evidently Thai food, both in Glasgow, and Singapore Sling in Edinburgh, make interesting assets to our range of food choices. There are, of course, examples of every kind of restaurant, Greek, Peruvian, Armenian, Mexican, Spanish, Japanese and Polish, in operation. One analogy for the difficulties under which they operate is to imagine the problems that would be encountered by expatriate Scots, setting up a Scottish restaurant in Mexico City or Corfu. It isn't an easy task, and some do it better than others. Ingredients are probably the least significant element in the equation. They lack a substantial, informed population of people who appreciate of what these cuisines consist, and as a consequence of that, miss a discriminating audience to keep them on their toes. Those who decide not to go down the well-worn path of turning out travesties adapted to local palates have to take on an educational role, which is another burden when it comes to establishing economic viability.

In Scotland, like the rest of the UK, the discerning burger-joint's room for manoeuvre is becoming, increasingly, more limited. The green consumer's ennui with red meat is growing, and the spread of the ungreen burger chains is capturing the bottom end of the market. So although restaurants like Di Maggio's and the Cul de Sac Crêperie in Glasgow can still offer an honest-to-goodness burger, the lure of everything else they have on the menu – pizza, pasta, crepes and so on – grows. The Tex-Mex/burger/American diner-school in Scotland is rapidly becoming a culinary backwater, with a marked over-reliance on bought-in catering products such as ersatz American pies and additive-laden puddings.

By comparison, the vegetarian and demi-vegetarian scene is growing. Serious restaurants in Edinburgh and Glasgow that don't have something thoughtful to offer this beleaguered, but growing minority, are increasingly out on a limb. The revolt against protein-intensive, over-rich food is reflected in changing menus. A large city hotel such as the Sheraton in Edinburgh now offers its diners an inspired 'Light Dining/Vegetarian menu'. And although some kitchens betray absolutely no awareness of politics of food issues by continuing to serve lightly cooked cattle offal in the peak of fears over BSE for example, more and more of the established city restaurants such as the Rogano in Glasgow, are showing a positive interest in serving organic vegetables and other products.

As mainstream restaurants wake up to the greening of food, they steal much of the thunder of the established vegetarian eating places. Significantly, some of the wholefood pioneers of the Seventies are showing signs of wear and tear, offering hessian food which works variations on a raw cabbage-leaden quiche-mayonnaise and bean theme. Perhaps they may yet wake up to the more sophisticated vegetarian palate that prevails in the Nineties. Amongst the more dedicated vegetarian outlets, Basil's in Glasgow and Seeds in Edinburgh are lively and dynamic representatives of our two cities' longstanding interest and commitment to vegetarian food – a permanent feature of the eating-out scene which only goes from strength to strength.

There are, of course, the one-off restaurants which don't fit any of the categories already mentioned. Jimmy's in Glasgow with its born-again fish and chips, Freed's also in Glasgow, offering Jewish home cooking; yet it is these broad categories of food discussed above which, I think, best represent the state of the art of eating out in our two major cities. When I started researching this book, I was full of misgivings about what I might uncover. In the event I was impressed by the number of good eating possibilities there were – far more than I had anticipated. I encountered few really bad meals and was often pleasantly surprised. This makes me all the more convinced that there is no reason or necessity for city residents or visitors ever to waste their money on poor food. Use this book and eat well!

BAMBOO GARDEN ♨

57a Frederick Street   031-225 2382

Head for the Bamboo Garden on Sunday lunchtimes. Leave Scotland behind as you descend the steep stairs into Hong Kong. Here you'll find the entire restaurant area chock-a-block with chattering tables of Chinese, family groups with even the tiniest babies in tow, or large groups of joking students. The temperature feels like Hong Kong too, with the build up of heat from the kitchen which is going full throttle and the pressure of so many bodies. Dim sum, (those delightful and varied Chinese appetisers which make the perfect lunch), are the thing. But so rare is it to see a non-Chinese face at this time, the extensive dim sum menu is printed only in Chinese. Don't be surprised if you are offered the standard Scottish menu. It does contain some dim sum, but nothing like the full range of possibilities. So hold your ground, and if all else fails (some staff speak a little English and you may feel almost bad about not speaking Chinese), point to what you see on the tables around you, nobody will mind. With a bit of negotiation, you can persuade the staff that you will enjoy what the Chinese are eating, despite their reservations! Having plugged yourself into the dim sum, sit back and sip tea . . . service is not fast, the place is so over-loaded. It is well worth the wait though. There are fresh rice rolls stuffed with fat prawns in soy and spring onions, or crab claws with shrimp paste, or clear chewy dumplings stuffed with beef and peanuts, or dainty vegetable rolls loaded with carrot and ginger or a steaming lotus leaf, concealing glutinous rice, char sui, duck and much, much more. Staff are friendly, if over-taxed, the atmosphere as stimulating as being in a foreign country. Dim sum as always, ridiculously cheap: two can eat a massive and interesting lunch for £10.

Restaurant information

Getting there: Bus – 80/29/28/C2
Open: Seven days; 12 noon–11.30p.m.
Price per head (average): £7.00–£10.00 (lunch) £12.00–£15.00 (dinner); Visa, Access and American Express cards accepted.
Facilities: Children welcome; smoking throughout.
Vegetarian food available.

BAR ROMA
39a Queensferry Street   031-226 2977

The victor in the bustling Italian bar-ristorante stakes, Bar Roma gets the popular block vote for fast, tasty Italian food at manageable prices. Outside, the narrow, curtained frontage does not prepare you for this huge, teeming restaurant with open kitchen which looks, smells and sounds like Italy. A telly flickers away in the corner, but no background music is needed because this is the sort of place that generates its own buzz. Food is served by the best sort of relaxed, competent and genial waiters who banter loudly in Italian amongst themselves in between cuddling babies and humming operatic arias. Bar Roma is a considerable operation, with an amazing throughput of bodies, especially family groups, and it is organised like clockwork. The food formula varies very little from many restaurants of its kind – Bar Roma is a relative of Bar Italia on Lothian Road – but the food here manages to taste better. Pasta and risotti come flexibly in either main or starter portions. You'll find the usual range of pastas (spaghetti vongole with clams, cannelloni and so on), with more unusual versions like rigatoni with spicy Norcina sausage and cream. The specials, written up on the board, are worth a second look. The gnocchi is wonderful, suitably starchy and filling with a great creamy tomato sauce and generous dustings of fresh parmesan. The pizzas are very respectable too, though purists may prefer to stick with tried and tested favourites like Margherita or Napoletana in preference to innovations such as tuna and banana. The menu includes more familiar trattoria dishes such as scalloppina Milanese, steak, scampi Provencale, but informal pasta and pizza dining seems more to the point. For a good value substantial snack, the crostini (toasted bread) topped with tomato sauce, mozzarella, fresher than usual dried herbs, fresh tomatoes and a generous lid of wafer-thin prosciutto, takes some beating. New wave Italian food has yet to touch Bar Roma – will it ever? Salads are the inevitable curly lettuce, tomato quarter, pepper slice and solitary olive type, desserts heavily reliant on bought-in ice-creams and cakes. Nearly fifty Italian wines to choose from, none of which is particularly cheap.

Restaurant information

Open: Seven days; 12 noon–2.00a.m.
Price per head (average): £8.00–£15.00; Visa and Mastercard accepted.
Facilities: Disabled toilet, children welcome; smoking throughout. Vegetarian food available.
Other services: Carry-out

BELL'S DINER 🍳
7 St Stephen Street   031-225 8116

Nothing much changes in St Stephen Street, that alternative chic
street which came to life in the 1970s and has remained much the
same since. Bell's Diner is no exception, a small affordable burger
joint with limited horizons, but good within those limits. Well-
made charcoal cooked burgers with a tasteful selection of
toppings, (the Roquefort has its devotees) and generous quantities
of home-made chips. Burgers are the heart of the matter, though
starters like mushrooms on toast are also a safe bet – just
straightforward freshly cooked mushrooms generously piled on
toast. The desserts are deeply unexciting . Wine choice is limited,
but unpretentious with bottles of Bulgarian Cabernet Sauvignon
at ungreedy prices. Reasonable diner-ish atmosphere, laid back
service – occasionally too slow.

Restaurant information

Getting there: Bus – 20/28/29/C3/80/34
Open: Seven days; Sun–Fri 6.00–10.30p.m. (last orders) Sat
11.00a.m.–10.30p.m. (last orders)
Price per head (average): £6.25–£10.25; No credit cards accepted.
Facilities: Wheelchair access, no disabled toilet; children welcome;
smoking throughout.
Vegetarian food available
Other services: Carry-out

CAFE BEAUMONT 🏠🏠
Sheraton Hotel, 1 Festival Square   031-229 9131

Chef Jean Michel Gauffre serves food which outstrips the norm for glitzy international hotels. A swift glance in the direction of the Cafe Beaumont might lead food lovers to think otherwise – the ambience is zooped-up department store coffee shop meets Crossroads Motel – and there is a confusing proliferation of menus. But this is cooking that caters capably for conventional palates, at the same time offering controlled innovation and some interesting options for those who look to life beyond steak, Dover sole and cheesecake. Lunchtime menus revolve around a help-yourself buffet, with a hot main course to structure it. It may sound ghastly, conjuring images of tired salmon and limp lettuce, but the reality is carefully made, savoury terrines and galantines (chicken and pistachio, lamb and venison, and salmon and halibut) which taste fresh, diverse and appetising. Roast beef and Yorkshire pudding makes an appearance on almost every menu from lunch to dinner to satisfy popular tastes, but you can just as well opt for pan-fried calf's liver flavoured with basil and olive oil, lobster pot au feu with star anise, smoked halibut and scampi tails with lime confit or casserole of hare with oyster mushrooms. Cooking is sure and well-executed with prevailing good taste. Any tendencies to couthie Scotchness encouraged by the high profile 'Taste of Scotland' menu, are kept firmly in check. The various menus change frequently, some daily, which adds interest. There is a light dining/vegetarian menu on offer with creative options like warm choux buns with wild mushroom casserole, tartare of salmon on a buckwheat pancake and smoked salmon and leek souffle – good news for jaded palates, which have seen too much protein and rich sauces. Carte prices are high but fair. Set lunches and dinners, which often throw in half bottles of wine with the price, represent very good value for money.

Restaurant information

Getting there: Bus – 16/10/9/11
Landmark: Sheraton Hotel, Usher Hall
Open: Seven days; 24 hours.
Price per head (average): £15.75 (lunch) £25.00 (dinner); all major credit cards accepted
Facilities: Wheelchair access; disabled toilet; children welcome; smoking in part.

CAFE NUMBER TWENTY-THREE 🍴

Catholic Chaplaincy Centre 23 George Square,
031-556 2618

A student cafe, open only in term-time offering a very limited menu of creative vegetarian dishes. Very basic surroundings, which fill up early. Main dish of the day might be a soupy dahl, accompanied by a flavoursome salad of softened but still crunchy cauliflower, seasoned with mustard seed and fresh coriander. Soups, like straight vegetable or French onion are hearty and wholesome. The kitchen runs to cakes for pudding – gooey chocolate or moist, cinnamony carrot. Theoretically service is at the table, but this is only if you operate by student time and can allow an hour and a half for lunch. The bright young things like a fag or two over coffee so it can get smoky . . . haven't they been listening to their guidance teachers?

Restaurant information

Getting there: Bus – 23/27/43
Open: Mon–Fri (University term time only); 10.00a.m.–5.00p.m.
Price per head (average): £1.50–£4.50; No credit cards accepted.
Facilities: No wheelchair access or disabled toilet; children welcome; smoking in part only.
Vegetarian food only.

CAFE ROYAL OYSTER BAR 🍽
17a West Register Street   031-556 4124

Not to be confused with the Cafe Royal Circle Bar or the public bar next door, the Cafe Royal Oyster Bar houses one of Edinburgh's most traditional restaurants. So special is the atmosphere of this well-tended Victorian bar with its original tiling, mirrors and panelling, that it has provided a popular backdrop for any number of films, adverts and interviews. Intense heat from the kitchen below warms the floor beneath your feet. The food formula is as unchanging as the setting. If you want fresh fish and shellfish, which has not been overly mucked around with, then it takes some beating. A traditional assertively smoked salmon comes from Lawrie's in Mallaig, native oysters from Colchester during the season, and giga oysters from Scotland during the summer. This is a classic menu – Dover sole, steak with béarnaise, lobster salad – with no concessions to modern or nouvelle cuisine. Sauces are mainly flour-based, but well-executed of their kind. The cheese board exhibits the shortcomings of traditionalism and the desserts are more or less an irrelevance. Bags of atmosphere, lots of famous faces to observe and fascinating conversations to eavesdrop.

Restaurant information

Landmark: Register House
Open: Seven days; 12 noon–2.00p.m. and 7.00–10.15p.m.
Price per head (average): £20.00–£30.00 (inc wine); Access and Visa cards accepted.
Facilities: Wheelchair access, no disabled toilet; children welcome; smoking throughout.
Vegetarian food available

CAFE SAINT-HONORE 🍴
34 Thistle Street Lane North   031-226 2211

The eponymous saint is 'Patron des Boulangers', in this case Edinburgh's well-loved French baker who hails from Brittany. The Boulangerie's bread is everywhere in the city, crunchy and crisp, with the authentic flavour which comes from imported French flour. The baker's café is reminiscent of the unremarkable but sound café/bars with food that you find all over France. The ambience is 100 per cent upgraded Paris bistro in the traditional style, with small tables set around the bar, cafe lights, paper tablecloths and tarnished mirrors. When staff greet you with a 'Bonjour', this is because they are unarguably French, not because they have been on a 'How To Behave Like A French Waiter' course. This is traditional mainstream French cooking, strong on good béchamel, winey reductions and sound fish stock. There are no surprises. Soups, French onion or fish, decent braises like boeuf Bourguignonne, grilled lemon sole, medallions of pork à l'orange, filled crêpes, crudités with aioli, stuffed mussels with garlic. Substantial salads include an okay salade niçoise or the classic goat cheese on toast which is let down by uninteresting salad leaves and lack-lustre vinaigrette. Otherwise, raddichio and Belgian chicory are the order of the day. Prices are acceptable but uneven – some dishes offer conspicuously better value for money than others. The Boulanger is also a pâtissier, so there is no shortage of classy pâtisserie to demolish with potent espresso coffee. The biscuity pâté sucrée tarts – like the amandine and cherry with crème pâtissiere – are the best. Professional service, a better than average selection of wines, and a properly stocked French bar.

Restaurant information

Getting there: Bus – 23/27
Open: Mon–Sat; 12 noon–2.30p.m. and 6.00–10.30p.m.
Price per head (average): £9.00 (lunch) £12.00 (dinner); Access and Visa cards accepted.
Facilities: wheelchair access, no disabled toilet; children welcome; smoking throughout.
Vegetarian food available.

CAPRICE PIZZARAMA 🍴
327 Leith Walk   031-554 1279/2430

The Caprice is so large, it is positively ungainly, a series of rooms and eating areas furnished in the unswinging Sixties genre. If this sounds unappealing, don't be put off, the style grows more attractive as the years go on. In amongst the vinyl seats, flock and hessian walls, stags heads, fish tanks, classical-ish figures in plaster *et al* is the food, which looks, and indeed tastes like standard trattoria fare with one big exception. The heart of the Caprice is its pine-fired brick pizza oven. You can stand and watch your pizza shaped and floured on a marble surface, then transferred on a pizza paddle to rise visibly in minutes before your eyes. The results are a base pizza, thin light and crisp, with a truly wonderful smoky taste. More sophisticated palates will yearn to provide their own toppings. The said toppings are pedestrian, (the pepperoni sausage one is probably the best), but the basic pizza base makes it all worthwhile. Other dishes are served in true Caprice style – heaped platefuls of fresh, if unexciting food at low prices. The sort of food to be savoured on a wet weekday night when you are starving and depressed by the size of your overdraft. Everything is served in children's portions, symptomatic of what is clearly a pro-child establishment, and there is a no-smoking room.

Restaurant information

Getting there: Bus – 7/87/16/17/C3/25/12
Open: Seven days; Mon–Sat 12 noon–2.00p.m. and 5.30–11.00p.m.; Sun 5.00–11.00p.m.
Price per head (average): £3.00–£7.50 (lunch) £10.00-£15.00 (dinner); all major credit cards accepted.
Facilities: Wheelchair access; no disabled toilet; children welcome; smoking in part only.
Vegetarian food available
Other services: Carry-out

CELLAR NO.1 ♙
1 Chambers Street   031-220 4298

One hesitates when describing Cellar No.1 as a wine bar – so often a euphemism for a jumped-up pub serving oxidised wines and bought-in catering food. Not so this joint venture of two of the city's noteworthy independent wine merchants – Wine Well and Howgate Wines. A steeply descending stair with an easy-to-miss entrance next to their shop at the seedy end of Chambers Street, leads you down to conspiratorial cellars. Hats off for creating a civilised and continental-ish environment in which to appreciate some serious wine and able food to go with it. On any day, at least twenty well-selected wines are on sale by the glass, kept fresh by dint of observant management, good turnover and the aid of vacuvin stoppers. You can also choose from the list of over 200 bottles. The food is a capable adjunct to the wine, offering a flexible, untrammelled approach depending on your mood. Some creative thinking has gone into light dishes in the under £2 bracket (baked Florence fennel with a saffron sauce, stir-fried green beans with crisp bacon, deep-fried potato skins with a surprisingly successful lemon sauce), all make great light lunches with bread and salad. More substantial dishes go for a hearty approach – cassoulet, mushroom stroganoff and the ever-popular spicy chicken strips. Cheeses could be a lot more exciting. Cellar No.1 regularly provokes compliments for its easy atmosphere and affordable good food. It is also refreshingly free from the usual wine bar hustle. Women on their own can, and do, drink and eat here without attracting funny looks or feeling uncomfortable.

Restaurant information

Getting there: Bus – 23/27/41/7/14/31/3/33
Landmark: Royal Scottish Museum
Open: Mon–Sat; Mon–Wed 11.00a.m.–midnight; Thurs–Sat 11.00a.m.–1.00a.m. Food served 12 noon–2.30p.m. and 6.00p.m.–10.00p.m. (later during Festival).
Price per head (average): £4.00–12.00; Access and Visa cards accepted.
Facilities: Smoking throughout.
Vegetarian food available

CITY CAFE 🍳
19 Blair Street   031-220 0125

This is one of Edinburgh's few actively stylish establishments. The style in question is Thirties American diner, in the unpretty tradition with lots of beaten metal, chrome, plastic, etched glass and hard surfaces. The crowd who are attracted to it, largely art students, architects and fellow travellers. There is a refreshing avoidance of kitsch nostalgia, though you can catch Lulu and Patsy Kline crooning (at a very low, almost subliminal level). Once upon a time, the City Cafe had aspirations to modern Italian food: carpaccio and so on. This clearly was not a winning formula for this market or location so it has settled down to a less ambitious level. The result is largely acceptable if unexciting food, served at decidedly low prices. The menu in keeping with its surroundings eschews unnecessary detail, so the set price lunch menu at under a fiver may simply state 'mushroom salad' without indicating that these are warm, fried, garlicky mushrooms on raddichio and endive, or fail to point out that the gruyère crêpe is coated in breadcrumbs and deep-fried. Plaice may turn out to be haddock, cooked in a nicely stewed red pepper and tomato sauce, vegetable bake, a sort of born again cauliflower cheese with a crisp, gratinated topping. Basics like bacon or steak sandwiches are generous and straightforward, though there are more modern dishes like a very decent tomato and feta salad at an unprecedented low price. Cappuccino or espresso coffee are powerful, though they have to fight hard to compete with the prevalent smell of floor polish which intensifies as you reach the back of the café. In the evening, the two non-ornamental fans whirr away but prove ineffectual in the face of an onslaught of bodies and chain-smokers. Service, on occasion, may be more moody, temperamental or hung-over than the customers.

Restaurant information

Landmark: Tron Kirk
Open: Seven days; Mon–Sat 12 noon–1.00a.m. Sun 12 noon–11.00p.m.
Price per head (average): £4.50 (lunch) £8.00–£9.00 (dinner).
Access and Visa cards accepted.
Facilities: Wheelchair access, disabled toilet; children welcome; smoking throughout.
Vegetarian food available

COURTHOUSE CAFE 🍴
Brodie's Close, 304 Lawnmarket

A safe house in prime tourist trap territory, this atmospheric café is within a stone's throw of the Castle. Despite the unpromising billboard which sits on the street to lure you into this historic High Street close, here is a refreshingly untwee space, designed in a simple, effective way. The effect of pewter torchlights suspended from the wall, old library-style lino and dado height wood panelling evokes history without being conventional. The management is studenty, amiable and articulate. The food formula is sensibly limited, (one suspects in the absence of core cooking skills). It does what it does well and refreshingly opts out of offering the bought-in catering garbage commonly encountered elsewhere. Soups – creamy mushroom, thick spicy lentil – are fine. So too, the leek and potato gratin with its bubbly cheesy crust. The now ubiquitous hot, stuffed croissant turns up, but in more interesting forms than usual (smoked ham and ricotta, brie and apple). Open sandwiches, like everything else here, are keenly priced – smoked salmon and cream cheese for the conformists or tuna, cashew nut and mayonnaise for the triers. Gaggia coffee and the opportunity to browse through the papers of the day make this a convivial place in which to while away some time.

Restaurant information

Getting there: Bus – 1/6/34/35/23/27/45/28/29/41/46/47/24/
Landmark: The Mound
Open: Tues–Sun; 10.00a.m.–6.00p.m. (winter) 10.00a.m.–10.00p.m. (summer)
Price per head (average): £3.00–£6.00; No credit cards accepted.
Facilities: Wheelchair access and disabled toilets; children welcome; smoking throughout.
Vegetarian food available

CHAN'S 🖻🖻
1 Forth Street   031-556 7118

Chinese restaurants in Britain are rarely fertile ground for vegetarians. Not so Chan's, which is remarkable in offering a page-long selection for this beleaguered, but growing, minority. What is more, the dishes are genuinely creative and different. Beancurd (tofu) every which way is one of the dominant ingredients, but for those who might otherwise feel that its wholesomeness is outweighed by its blandness, here's a range of dishes to challenge your prejudices. Deep-fried dainty conical balls of beancurd, sweet corn, spring onion and carrot come with a hot fermented black bean sauce, or more simply cooked with cashew nuts and mushrooms. There is a fine glutinous hot and sour soup minus the meat, full of juicy sliced Chinese mushrooms. Deep-fried cucumber comes in a triumphant light, crisp, almost tempura-like batter with a chilli and garlic flavoured satay dipping sauce. Seasonal vegetables in the Szechuan style consists of demonstrably fresh green pepper, celery, baby corn, freshly roasted cashews and wood ear mushrooms with a slightly sweet and delicious sesame sauce. Presentation is a strong point – the dishes are tasteful yet colourful. Even the rice is exceptional, shiny, separate highly polished and perfumed grains which suggest the top grade. Meat-eaters are well-treated too, but the excitement of the vegetables is hard to ignore. Tropical fish and red silk provide a familiar backdrop for both Scottish and Chinese diners. Prompt service, delightfully low prices.

Restaurant information

Getting there: Bus – 7/14/10/37
Open: Wed–Mon; 5.30p.m.–midnight. Lunch 12 noon–2.00p.m. Fridays only
Price per head (average): £3.70 (lunch) £6.50–£10.00 (dinner); Access, Visa and American Express cards accepted.
Facilities: Children welcome; smoking throughout.
Vegetarian food available
Other services: Carry-out

DORIC TAVERN ♟♟
15 Market Street   031-225 1084

For those who are not in the know, the Doric looks relatively unpromising from the outside, a feeling that is not alleviated by the spartan feel of this bistro bar once inside. There's a sense that this should only be another unremarkable wine bar, serving staple wine-bar fare. So it is a bonus to find out that the cooking is cosmopolitan (in the complimentary sense) and that the kitchen takes a commitment to freshness and good basic ingredients as its starting point. A note from the head chef on the menu tips you off to the house philosophy – 'We're moving towards organic meat, poultry and vegetables, the regular supply of which is hard to secure and in many cases prohibitively expensive at present. However we seek to pay more than lip service to these over the coming weeks.' Rich pickings here for everyone, especially vegetarians or demi-veggies. Aubergine parmigiana is well done (the kitchen makes a good tomato sauce), there's good skewered vegetables with a satay sauce, and stuffed baked crab makes the ideal light lunch. More expensive options centre on fish – often scallops, sardines, tuna – cooked straightforwardly (grilled sole with chive butter) or more innovatively (shark stir-fried with anise and fennel). For meat eaters, there's stir-fried chicken flavoured with lemon grass and fresh chilli, pork fillet with creamed clams and tomatoes and more to choose from. Service is never the strength here and the kitchen shows signs of strain during busy periods, with hastily prepared dishes. Proximity to Scotsman Publications Ltd ensures a regular journalistic clientèle.

Restaurant information

Landmark: The Fruitmarket Gallery
Open: Mon–Sat, Sunday evening during the Festival; food served 12 noon –2.30p.m. and 6.00–10.30p.m.
Price per head (average): £6.95 (lunch) £8.00–10.00 (dinner); Access, Visa and American Express cards accepted.
Facilities: Children welcome if supervised; smoking throughout. Vegetarian food available

DUBH PRAIS 🍴🍴
123b High Street 031-557 5732

Down an easy-to-miss stair off the High Street, you'll find this neat, bright restaurant where chef-proprietor James McWilliams serves a limited range of classical dishes which rest on good fresh ingredients and thorough execution. Culinary certificates decorate the wall, but even if you missed these, you'd notice that there was a sure hand in the kitchen when the food arrives. There is nothing modern about the menu; this is the place for traditional favourites. Options include good smoked salmon, a sound cock-a-leekie or smoked haddock soup, or a light pheasant and watercress mousse. Renditions are simple (fat shelled prawns with garlic butter, sole bonne femme, steak with mustard sauce) and there is none of the over-elaboration associated with much contemporary chef cooking. Fluffy white fillets of sole come gratinated under a properly cooked, winey mornay sauce, chicken moist and juicy in a well-reduced apple and onion sauce. A pale and uncommercial grilled smoked haddock arrives refreshingly unadorned. Vegetables are conventional – steamed broccoli, green beans, sauté potatoes *et al* – but are fresher and more sensitively cooked than usual. The menu plays on the Taste of Scotland theme but has enough respect for ingredients to avoid gratuitous tartan clichés, so there's saddle of hare with Drambuie sauce, game casserole or duck with bramble sauce. Desserts, like everything here, are simply and attractively presented and range from a home-made parfait of creamy chocolate ice-cream with pistachios and lashings of alcohol to blackberry shortcake. Invigorating coffee follows, a welcome deviation from the stewed filter mould. Not a restaurant for those who value excitement and adventure, but a winner for conventional palates who like simple things decently done.

Restaurant information

Landmark: John Knox's House
Open: Tues–Sat; 12 noon–2.15p.m. and 6.30–10.30p.m.
Price per head (average): £7.00 (lunch) £15.00 (dinner); American Express, Visa and Access cards accepted.
Facilities: Children welcome; smoking throughout.
Vegetarian food available

DUNCAN'S LAND 🍺🍺🍺
8 Gloucester Street   031-225 1037

Small, and some may think pretty, family-run Italian restaurant which distinguishes itself by offering an even performance from start to finish. At lunch it caters for the business community, though not for that variety who come for the port and cigars or to impress their clients. This is good Italian restaurant food with elements of hearty home-cooking grafted on. The menu is small and changes every two months or so, and the lunch-time one constitutes a bargain. Starters can include a garlicky, tomato risotto (sadly not with arborio rice but good nevertheless), loaded with fat, tasty, fresh mussels, or dainty squares of polenta with melted gorgonzola. A dish of small dab sole, cooked in a winey, tomato flecked sauce makes a good main course, especially when the vegetables arrive. This is a kitchen that takes its vegetables seriously to admirable effect – eggy cauliflower fritters, gratin potatoes flavoured with rosemary and topped with crunchy breadcrumbs and lemon zest plus a good mélange of carrot, leek and courgette. Simple pasta dishes are well done. Silky tagliatelle comes in a well-reduced cream sauce, subtly flavoured with sweet sweated onions. There are lots of clear, assertive flavours and nothing is bland, although the chef cooks with a light hand. For once, there is respite from the bought-in ice-cream desserts on which so many Italian eateries rely. In their place, a formidable, towering zuppa inglese with an inch thick layer of vanilla custard, a good dark crema caramela or an alcoholic tiramisu. Wines are unexciting basic Italian, coffee suitably potent and continental. Fast, pleasant service with a soft spot for children.

Restaurant information

Getting there: Bus – 28/29/C3/80/34
Landmark: Stockbridge Health Centre
Open: Tues–Sat; 12.30–2.00p.m (last orders) and 6.30–10.00p.m. (last orders). Not open for lunch on Saturday.
Price per head (average): £7.50 (lunch) £15.00 (dinner); Visa and Access cards accepted.
Facilities: Wheelchair access, no disabled toilet; children welcome; smoking throughout.

FERRI'S

1 Antigua Street   031-556 5592

A basic, unassuming Italian restaurant, much loved by night-hawks – it stays open until 3.00 a.m. This is a place where, with some astute selection, you can eat very well. The pasta dishes are hearty and wholesome, pizzas crisp and yeasty, but it is still very definitely yesterday's Scottish-Italian food. Peas are tinned, herbs are dried, and desserts consist almost exclusively of commercial ice-cream. But for weekday comfort food at low prices, Ferri's takes some beating. A plate of penne with spicy sausage, or pasticiatta – a composite dish of pasta, bolognese sauce, peas and cream – will raise your spirits. The garlic bread, a pizza base rubbed with oil, herbs and liberally anointed with the said garlic, is not to be missed. Invariably busy, with a mixed clientele and a definite buzz.

Restaurant information

Getting there: Bus – 9/10/15/16/11/44/4/5/26/21/12
Landmark: Playhouse Theatre
Open: Seven days; Mon–Thurs 12 noon–3.00a.m., Fri–Sat 12 noon–4.00a.m., Sun 12 noon–2.00a.m.
Price per head (average): £3.50–£6.00 (lunch) £8.00 (dinner); Access, Visa, Diners and American Express cards accepted.
Facilities: children welcome; smoking throughout
Vegetarian food available
Other services: Home delivery and carry-out.

THE INDIAN CAVALRY CLUB 🍴🍴
3 Atholl Place   031-228 3282

This is one of Edinburgh's new wave Indian restaurants, easy to miss behind its drab and lack-lustre frontage. Inside, light and airy decor with wooden blinds and simple calico swags transports you into a cool 'heat and dust' atmosphere, effectively blotting out the remorseless flow of traffic outside. Dashing waiters in cavalry gear go down well with the junior members of the party, and offer efficient and affable service. The cooking is stimulating and special, with subtle flavours and intriguing nuances. Each dish has its own distinctive flavour whether it is creamy chicken makhani in a gentle, buttery sauce or green herb lamb, fragrant with still distinct spring onions and coriander. Vegetarian options, such as peppery spinach with curd cheese, or steamed vegetables with fresh chilli, coriander leaves and lentils are no second best. Both rice and bread are fresh and light. Depending on availability, there's an exotic fresh fruit cocktail to round things off. You wait just long enough to feel assured that your food is actually being prepared on the spot, not microwaved.

Restaurant information

Open: Seven days; 12 noon–2.30p.m. and 5.30–11.30p.m.
Price per head (average): £5.95 (lunch) £12.95 (dinner); Visa, American Express, Access and Diners cards accepted.
Facilities: Wheelchair access, no disabled toilet; children welcome; smoking in part.
Vegetarian food available
Other services: Carry-out and home delivery.

KALPNA 🍴🍴🍴
2–3 St Patrick Square   031-667 9890

The Kalpna holds a unique place in the forefront of Indian and vegetarian food, not just in Scotland but in Britain. Since Dik Mehta opened it along with his chef and now partner Ajay Bharatdwaj over nine years ago, it has established itself as an outstanding, no-compromise Indian restaurant with a commitment to authenticity which has never been in question. The cuisine is Gujerati and therefore vegetarian. If there is a vegetarian Nirvana, then this must be it. No surprise then, that the Kalpna regularly wins accolades on the vegetarian front. This is not to imply that carnivores will be disappointed: with a kitchen as sophisticated and skilled as the Kalpna's, meat just won't be missed. Here you will find the complete antithesis of the infamous 'International Sauce'. In its place, subtle and delicious herbing, plenty of texture and contrast, complex and intriguing flavours. To start, it is hard to look further than the lentil kachoris – deliciously mealy, spiced lentils inside a light crust – or bhel poori, hot and sweet potatoes studded with raisins inside a puffed rice ball. A light tamarind sauce accompanies. Sweet and sour flavours are played on in main dishes like the vegetable cutlets or stir-fried vegetables flavoured with cream and coriander. Navratan kurma, a mixture of vegetables and nuts in a creamy piquant sauce, has

built up a following of its own. Likewise, the speciality Khoya Kaju, the chef's inspired invention where reduced cream, sultanas, pistachio and nutmeg are combined to riveting effect. Breads are brilliantly light and airy, whether you go for the delightfully puffy pooris or a delicate paratha stuffed with curd cheese, onions and black pepper. Standards do not relent at dessert. Everything is home-made right down to the ice-cream and sorbets. If carrot halva scented with cardamom does not draw you, the mango or nut and spice kulfi (Indian ice-cream) will. The atmosphere and decor are in harmony with the cooking. There is no appeal to fond imperialistic notions of India, no militaria or whirring fans, instead plain walls adorned only with modern Indian art. The restaurant's policy is no-smoking, which obviously endears it to its clientele: non-stuffy but well behaved cosmopolitan city dwellers with a slightly disproportionate representation of academics (by virtue of its proximity to the university).

Restaurant information

Getting there: Bus – 3/5/8/14/33/69/87
Landmark: Odeon Cinema
Open: Mon–Sat; Mon–Fri 12 noon–2.00p.m. and 5.30p.m.–11.00p.m., Sat 5.30p.m.–11.00p.m.
Price per head (average): £3.00 (lunch) £9.00 (dinner); Visa and Access cards accepted.
Facilities: Wheelchair access, no disabled toilet; children welcome; no smoking.
Exclusively vegetarian
Other services: Carry-out

KELLY'S ♙

46 West Richmond Street   031-668 3847

Take careful note of the street number or you are likely to miss this discreet, family-run restaurant. The decor is pink and feminine, almost boudoir-like. The fare, standard dinner party stuff in the modern tradition, is executed for the main part with a sure hand. It is the sort of food that attracts a certain kind of respectable AB1 clientele – doctors discuss their patients, accountants' wives share grumbles. The wine list is unquestioningly passed to male members of the party, and wine proffered to them to taste. Other irritating characteristics include what appear to be arbitrary supplements on certain dishes, not a major concern in the midst of what is conspicuously formidable value for money. Food is good and, word has it, reliable – an intense, sweetish onion soup with a robust stock base, tender pheasant braised in red wine flavoured with ham and orange – though there are a few lapses of taste. Does tomato and basil sorbet add anything to a plate of smoked salmon; do parsley sprigs improve a souffle? Predictably, you are spoilt for choice when it comes to desserts which approach ten on occasion, including lemon roulade with lemon sauce, kiwi sorbet, orange tart with tayberry glaze.

Restaurant information

Getting there: Bus – 3/31/33/14/7/87/80/C3
Landmark: Surgeons' Hall
Open: Tues–Sat; 6.45–9.45p.m. (last orders)
Price per head (average): £16.00; Access, Visa and American Express cards accepted.
Facilities: Wheelchair access, disabled toilet; children welcome; no smoking before 9.00p.m.
Vegetarian food available

KWEILIN 🍴
19–21 Dundas Street   031-557 1752

Slick and polished Cantonese eatery, which seems permanently full of vociferous tableloads of office workers on the work night out. Glitzy, well-run and with the sort of turnover and throughput of customers which bodes well for freshness. The menu in English with French headings 'Dim sum et Hors D'oeuvres' is mainstream Cantonese and wholly predictable but reliable at that, without obvious evidence of the ubiquitous 'white powder' (monosodium glutamate). Once experienced the spiced and salted pork ribs are addictive, lean pork flavoured pungently and effectively with chilli, garlic and salt. Singapore noodles, full of what one imagines must be a representative cross-section of everything that passes through the kitchen, lend authenticity. Crispy aromatic duck has been dull and disappointing on occasion. Curiosities like crunchy water chestnut pudding, a sort of Chinese junket, provide a contrast to pedestrian staples like banana fritters. Front of house staff are friendly and patient.

Restaurant information

Getting there: Bus – 23/27
Open: Seven days; Mon–Thurs 12 noon–11.00p.m., Fri–Sat 12 noon–11.30p.m., Sun 5.00p.m.–11.00p.m.
Price per head (average): £10.00 (lunch) £15.00 (dinner); Access and Visa cards accepted
Facilities: smoking throughout
Vegetarian food available
Other services: discreet carry-out service available.

LA CUISINE D'ODILE 🐌🐌
French Institute, 13 Randolph Crescent   031-225 5366

Hidden away in the basement of this little bit of France in Edinburgh, you will find La Cuisine d'Odile. The eponymous Odile produces that admirable strain of real French home-cooking which is almost never encountered in Britain. It is open for full meals at lunch-time only and vastly popular, so reservation, if not block-booking is the name of the game. Staple dishes include a remarkable quiche,(which puts the commercial ones on offer elsewhere to shame), served with crisp crudités, or a well-dressed salade composée with nuts and cubes of various cheeses. More substantial courses range from a light lamb, pearl barley and vegetable stew flavoured with fresh mint or buttery sole with herbs and waxy potatoes. Pastry is divine. A crumbly pâte brisée redcurrant tart filled with crème pâtissière is beyond reproach. There are a couple of tables outside for balmy days. Terrific value for money.

Restaurant information

Getting there: All buses to the West end of Princes Street
Landmark: The French Institute
Open: Mon–Fri; 12 noon–2.00p.m. Closed July, Christmas and Easter holidays.
Price per head (average): £5.00; No credit cards accepted.
Facilities: Smoking throughout.
Vegetarian food available

LAIGH KITCHEN ♙
117a Hanover Street   031-225 1552

Anyone who wants to lend weight to the view that Edinburgh never changes need look no further than the Laigh. Since it moved down the hill into its basement premises some years back, it seems preserved in aspic. The formula is a winning one, so why change it and risk the wrath of the regulars who like things exactly as they are? Home-made soup, a selective choice of filling salads (tuna, rice and mayonnaise has its devotees), well-raised scones, oatcakes and lavish baking are the order of the day. Expatriates dream of the hazelnut meringue in distant climes. The setting is a white-washed basement furnished with antiques of the unflashy kind, and a couthie Scottish atmosphere. The manner of service is traditional, if not entirely flexible. This is the sort of place that has rules for the good of all and omnipresent signs to back them up of the 'please do this and not that' variety. All this can be slightly trying for stray visitors who are not club members.

Restaurant information

Getting there: Bus – 23/27/89
Landmark: Queen Street Gardens
Open: Mon–Sat; 8.30a.m.–4.00p.m. (5.00p.m. during the Festival)
Price per head (average): £5.00; No credit cards accepted.
Facilities: Children welcome; smoking in part
Vegetarian food available

LANCERS BRASSERIE 🍴
5 Hamilton Place   031-332 3444

There is not much to choose between Lancers, and restaurants like the Verandah at Haymarket and the Raj at Leith, which go to make up the second division of Indian restaurants in the city. Though they lack the edge of restaurants like the Kalpna or Shamiana, they still offer a sound basic standard, which is reliable and value for money. Lancers has a casual air and a social worker/teacherish clientele, the sort of people who are eating out with their own hard-earned money, and doing so reasonably frequently. The cooking is said to be Bengali, and ranges over the staple tandoori dishes and favourites like lamb pasanda with its mild, almondy sauce. As always, vegetarians are in their element and have perhaps, the most interesting dishes to choose from whether it be cabbage rolls stuffed with curd cheese or hot mixed vegetables with lentils. The cooking for the main part is able, but sauces, though ungreasy tend to resemble one another. There is a conspicuous lack of whole spices, and the menu is fond of flowery descriptions which sometimes don't make it to the plate. There is a French menu – Poulet Lancers, Crevettes Provencales – for those who want it. Indian ice-cream (kulfi) is rich and delicious but not enhanced with multi-colour sprinkles. Lancers does a thriving takeaway trade.

Restaurant information

Getting there: Bus – 28/29/C3/80/34/35
Landmark: Theatre Workshop
Open: Seven days; 12 noon–2.30p.m. and 5.30–11.30p.m.
Price per head (average): £5.95 special buffet lunch. Dinner £8.95 (Vegetarian) 11.95 (Non-vegetarian); Access, Visa and American Express cards accepted.
Facilities: Wheelchair access, no disabled toilet; children welcome; smoking throughout.
Vegetarian food available

LA POTINIÈRE 🏠🏠🏠

Main Street, Gullane (On the A198 approximately 18 miles from Edinburgh)   0620 843214

Few restaurants in Scotland receive the consistent critical acclaim attracted by Hilary and David Brown's small and unobtrusive restaurant on Gullane's douce main street. This is classical French cooking, in a limited repertoire, executed perfectly with no technical faults. Hilary Brown's flavours are deep and well-judged. In totality a fairly rich formula which makes ideal material for the occasional grande bouffe. There is a discernible pattern. A sound soup (potage St Germain or carrot and mint for example), followed by an intermediate course such as mousselines of chicken or smoked fish anointed with fresh tomato, basil and virgin olive oil. To follow, rosy pink slices of beef fillet in the ultimate madeira sauce or breast of pigeon with wild morel mushrooms and green lentils, or a juicy tarragon chicken, perhaps. Accompaniments favour an unfussy, traditional approach – irreproachable gratin dauphinoise, a good green salad. A slice of brie with apple next, by this stage both unnecessary and unexciting and so to dessert, the sort of desserts that inspire fond memories. There's a beautifully textured orange soufflé glacé with caramelised orange or the definitive petit pot au chocolat and other treasures in this vein. David Brown's keen and long-lived interest in wine shows in his list which is extensive, full of old vintages and offered (like the food) at generous prices. This is the sort of wine list that it is silly not to take full advantage of. . . . hard lines on the person who draws the driving short straw. Despite the fact that La Potinière tends to be booked well in advance, experience shows that chasing after cancellations can allow you to jump the queue.

Restaurant information

Open: Six days, closed Wednesday; lunch 1.00p.m. Mon, Tues, Thurs, Sun; dinner 8.00p.m. Fri and Sat.
Price per head (average): £14.50 (lunch) £21.50 (dinner); no credit cards accepted.
Facilities: Wheelchair access, no disabled toilet; children welcome; no smoking.
Vegetarian food by prior arrangement

L'AUBERGE 🍴🍴🍴
58 St Mary's Street   031-556 5888

L'Auberge is no newcomer to the Edinburgh restaurant scene, but of late, under the watchful eye of proprieter Daniel Wencker, it seems to be putting on a winning performance. Everything about the place suggests that this is a restaurant which is deadly serious about success, out to get a Michelin star even. And if recent standards can be maintained and consolidated, this may not prove unrealistic. The ambience is unreservedly French, decor comfortable luxurious in the modern French style (with the odd silly bit of etiquette like 'Ladies Menus' without prices). Front of house service is French and polished, wines are French (Burgundies are extensive) with a few token Australians thrown in. The cooking (surprise, surprise) is French in influence, definitely nouvelle cuisine, but well-understood and accomplished in its rendition. Presentation shows flair and style without prissy tendencies. Carte starters include superior salades tièdes with ingredients like plump, firm langoustines, wild mushrooms, good salad leaves and judiciously balanced vinaigrettes. Classic dishes are delightfully done too – a truffled chicken liver mousse is special enough to evoke the flavours of fresh fois gras – and the home made brioche which accompanies it is perfect. There are points of excitement,

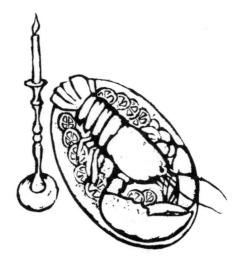

such as a magnificent home-made confit of duck, with its fat crisply rendered, its meat tender and unctuous. Sauces are masterful, tastefully judged with all elements working in harmony. Fine fish (Dover sole, wild salmon) make stunning appearances, and in common with the meat, are cooked with precision. Side vegetables are simple, but delicately done and there are interesting raw marinated vegetable garnishes to be had. There is a narrow but discerning choice of French artisan cheeses – Brie de Meaux, Explorateur, Fourme d'Ambert and the like – but the desserts take centre stage. There are elaborate concoctions on the raspberry theme (a roulade, a bavaroise, tiny buttery sables) served with a sharp orange sauce or an avant garde looking pavé of chocolate mousses with featherlight honey biscuits, Normandy Apple tart with caramel sauce and more. In keeping with its aspirations and performance, L'Auberge charges London prices, and the wines are ferociously expensive. There are however set lunch and dinner menus, offering the same standard food in a more limited vein, which represent excellent value for money.

Restaurant information

Landmark: Royal Mile
Open: Seven days; 12.15–2.00p.m. and 6.15 -9.30p.m.
Price per head (average): £8.00–£20.00 (lunch) £17.00–£20.00 (dinner); Access, Visa, American Express and Diners cards accepted.
Facilities: Wheelchair access, no disabled toilets; children welcome; smoking throughout.
Vegetarian food available

LOBBY LOUNGE ♙
Sheraton Hotel, 1 Festival Square   031-229 9131

Though some may find the glitzy formula international hotel decor too crass for comfort, it has to be accepted that the central lobby in the Sheraton has its uses, particularly in Lothian Road which otherwise fields an indifferent team of eateries. It remains open until midnight (twenty-four hours for residents) serving a much-better-than-average selection of sandwiches and open sandwiches. The formidable Sheraton triple-deck sandwich is generous in the American way and will easily feed two. The lobby is mindlessly comfortable and teeming with life, of the kind that evokes the opening sequences of Seventies disaster movies before calamity hits. The service is fast but you can sit around for ages without feeling under pressure. There is an easy-listening lobby pianist around 9.00 p.m. if you need some soothing. Free car-parking in the Sheraton's car-park makes it doubly attractive and well worth the inflated price of a coffee, though other tariffs are not unreasonable.

Restaurant information

Getting there: Bus – 16/10/9/11
Landmark: Sheraton Hotel
Open: Seven days; 7.00–10.00a.m. (breakfast) 11.00a.m.–11.00p.m. (Menu and beverages) 11.00p.m.–7.00a.m. limited.
Price per head (average): £4.00 (lunch) £4.00 (dinner); Visa, Access, American Express and Diners cards accepted.
Facilities: Wheelchair access, disabled toilet; children welcome; smoking in part.
Vegetarian food available

LOON FUNG 🍶
2 Warriston Place   031-556 1781/557 0940

The Loon Fung is the original Edinburgh Cantonese restaurant. Massively popular,(especially with impecunious middle-class families), it has built up over the years a loyal following for unreformed Chinese-Scottish food of the mouth-mugging sweet and sour/lemon chicken variety. Clearly, this is still a successful formula which the Loon Fung dares not change without risking the wrath of its clients. Newer (possibly more authentic) dishes are creeping on to the menu, like crispy lemon duck, chicken coated with flaked almonds and orange, Szechuan or Korean style beef and fried oysters. Fresh seafood has penetrated the establishment, as witnessed by a generous slice of pearly steamed halibut topped with fermented black beans and chilli. Or there is still protesting fresh lobster deliciously enhanced with spring onions and ginger. Monkfish and Dover sole are other favourites to be had, though their arrival has not spelt the death knell for the frozen abalone. The menu is far too long and could do with a drastic pruning. Dim sum are not the best to be had in the city. Vegetarians are in difficulties with meaty protein in some form fairly hard to avoid and bland vegetable stir-fries hardly worth the effort.

Getting there: Bus – 23/27/8/9/39
Open: Seven days; Mon–Thurs 12 noon–midnight, Fri 12 noon–1.00a.m., Sat 2.00p.m.–1.00a.m., Sun 2.00p.m.–midnight
Price per head (average): £4.50 (lunch) £9.00–£13.50 (dinner); Access, Visa and American Express cards accepted.
Facilities: Wheelchair access, no disabled toilets; children welcome; no smoking.
Vegetarian food available
Other services: Carry-out

LORENZO'S ♟

5 Johnston Terrace   031-226 2426

A relative newcomer to the Edinburgh ristorante scene, Lorenzo's is the first of the city's more casual Italian eateries to show awareness that the world has moved on from standard trattoria fare. The menu states explicitly where seafood is fresh and oil extra virgin. Superficially, this is a familiar menu, competently executed, but there are points of interest. Arancini di riso, croquettes of arborio rice bound with mozzarella and parmesan then deep-fried rate an alpha, as are the thin straws of courgette which are also deep-fried, but this time in a light and clean tasting batter. House specialities include an interesting stuffed manicotti with ricotta cheese and spinach. Up-market offerings span fillets of sole poached in white wine and cream with pine kernels and raisins or pan-fried liver and pancetta deglazed with white wine, with more in between. Regulars, however, may find it hard to move on from the house Foccacia – a rustic, crackling-crisp pizza base loaded with oregano, garlic and coarse salt. As for ambience, Lorenzo (whoever he may be) has abandoned the candle-in-the-Chianti-bottle school of interior design. Calm black and white photos of Italian cities cover the walls – except in the toilets which are papered with pages from Corriera de la Serra. Otherwise classically-inspired wall murals and music are the order of the day. On fine days there is provision for eating out of doors.

Exceptional value for money, especially when you consider that Lorenzo's is just around the corner from the Castle. Actively charming service of the flexible and efficient variety in tandem with a lightning kitchen. Plenty of time for children.

Restaurant information

Open: Seven days; 12 noon–11.00p.m.
Price per head (average): £8.00 (lunch) £10.00 (dinner); all major credit cards accepted.
Facilities: Children welcome; smoking throughout.
Vegetarian food available
Other services: Carry-out

LOWER AISLE 🏠

St Giles Cathedral, High Street (Royal Mile)   031-225 5147

Hidden away in the basement below St Giles' Cathedral, this lunch-time restaurant is quintessentially Edinburgh. All the elements are there. Traditional setting (historic church, aged vaults), discreet entrance (easy to miss), unflashy good taste (flag stones, simple wood furniture), with a clientele composed of that peculiarly Edinburgh blend of lawyers, councillors, journalists and local government officials. The food is traditional in the best sense of the word, simple, unfussy and great value for money. While you eavesdrop the fascinating conversations around and update yourself on the latest transgressions of the Scottish judiciary you can sup a bowl of lentil or split pea soup just like granny's. As conversation drifts on to the senior partner's irritating habits, there are generous servings of the dish of the day, which tend to be dishes like kedgeree, fish or cottage pie, all executed to a remarkably high standard. No truly Edinburgh eating place is complete without baking, and here the Lower Aisle particularly excels. You name it – Bakewell tart, millionaire's shortbread, border tart, iced shortcake, ginger biscuits, paradise slice – no sooner said than eaten. Coffee, like everything else here is sensible, served in cups or mugs as you prefer. Avoid the one o' clock rush.

Restaurant information

Getting there: Bus – 6/35/23/27/45/46/34/29/28/40/41
Landmark: St Giles' Cathedral
Open: Sun–Fri (Saturday during the Festival); Mon–Fri 10.00a.m.–4.30p.m., Sun 10.00a.m.–1.30p.m.
Price per head (average): £2–£2.50; no credit cards accepted.
Facilities: Wheelchair access; no disabled toilet; children welcome; smoking in part.
Vegetarian food available

MAMMA'S ♙
28–30 The Grassmarket   031-225 6464

Pizza is not exactly a high performance category in Edinburgh. Here in the Grassmarket, one of the traditional centres for the Italian community, the onus falls on Canadians to produce a pizza to compete with the famous Caprice in Leith Walk. Half a takeaway and half a restaurant, Mamma's pizzas emerge from a seriously professional-looking gas-fired pizza oven. Although some might argue that they miss the featherweight, wood smoky pizza bases to be had at the Caprice, the toppings at Mamma's are light years ahead. You select a basic pizza with tomato and mozzarella which comes in three sizes and choose your own toppings (thirty-seven to be precise) which include sun-dried tomatoes, capers, asparagus, prosciutto, and haggis – for those who like gimmicks. The restaurant area is blue gingham checked and fun in a sort of North American adolescent way. Pizzas form the core but there are a number of okay if unexciting puddings of the brownies and ice-cream variety to be had. The management likes to project its personality. Guidance on service charges runs as follows: 'The staff love it when you chuck money at them'. Similarly, 'The music is generally loud' states the menu 'If it is too loud, please complain. . . . but don't expect us to turn it down much because then we wouldn't be hip and we hate not being hip'. So if you find Neil Diamond playing at full blast a bit hard to take, better to opt for a pizza to go.

Restaurant information

Open: Seven days; Mon–Thurs 3.00p.m.–midnight, Fri–Sat 12 noon–1.00a.m., Sun 1.00–10.00p.m.
Price per head (average): £7.00; no credit cards accepted.
Facilities: Wheelchair access, disabled toilet; children welcome; smoking throughout.
Vegetarian food available
Other services: Home delivery and carry-out.

MARTIN'S ♟♟♟
70 Rose Street North Lane   031-225 3106

Here's a small, unflashy restaurant which is rapidly consolidating its reputation as the best, and most reliable site for serious food in the modern mood in Edinburgh. Almost buried alive in the warehousing at the back of Princes Street, Martin and Gay Iron's restaurant reflects their personalities – relaxed and unpretentious. The carpet was green long before the philosophy was consciously so, but the message comes over loud and clear with organic vegetables and house wine, an emphasis on wild ingredients – salmon, venison, rosehip, nettles, elderflowers – and an uncompromising array of unpasteurised artisan cheeses with a Scottish emphasis, invariably in prime condition. The positive emphasis on wholesomely sourced products is reinforced by eschewing foods which are reared exploitatively or inhumanely: you won't find broiler chicken on this menu. Getting the ideology right is one thing but you can't eat words. Thankfully, there are no worries in this department because chef David Macrae's cooking is sure, innovative in the good sense. His approach is light, he knows where to stop, avoiding the pitfall of over-elaboration which dogs so many chefs working in the same genre. The personnel in this kitchen hardly changes, making for dependable results. Warm salads, which work on many permutations (chorizo, avocado and pine kernel, rare pigeon breast, bacon, waxy potatoes) are unfailingly good. Some magnificent fresh fish passes through the kitchen – sea bass, brill, turbot are favourites – tastefully enhanced with an intense sea urchin sauce perhaps, or Japanese rice vinegar and vinegar marinade. Martin's is not cheap, but few will quibble with food of this standard. The set lunch offers great value.

Restaurant information

Open: Tues–Sat; Tues–Fri 12 noon–2.00p.m. and 7.00–10.00p.m. Not open for lunch Sat.
Price per head (average): £11.75 (lunch excluding wine) £23.00 (dinner excluding wine); Access and Visa cards accepted.
Facilities: Children over 10 years welcome; smoking in bar area only. Vegetarian food on request

MR V's
7 Charlotte Lane   031-220 0176

A stone's throw away from much-loved Bar Roma, Mr V's appeals to those who want middle to upper range British-Italian food in less frantic and bustling surroundings. The setting is almost rustic, a cobbled courtyard (magnificent for sunny days) or the low-roofed, more claustrophobic restaurant upstairs. Clientele tends to be of the muted business variety, who appreciate good service and being fussed over a bit, but also being processed in good time. There are good salads in the modern style – spinach with walnuts, croutons and bacon or tomato with fresh basil and mozzarella – and more familiar variations on Parma ham and avocado lines. You can eat a relatively inexpensive dish of pasta and pesto perhaps, or splash out on the fish of the day. There are interesting options, such as rabbit cooked in red wine, fillets of sole with pine kernels and sultanas or thin slices of carpaccio dressed with parmesan shavings and lemon juice. Great emphasis is laid on service – the management prides itself in catering to the customer's requests – and so it has a regular following.

Restaurant information

Getting there: All buses to the West end of Princes Street
Open: Mon–Sat; 12 noon–2.00p.m. and 6.30–11.00p.m.
Price per head (average): £8.50 (lunch) £15.00 (dinner); Diners, Visa, Access and American Express cards accepted.
Facilities: Children welcome; smoking throughout.
Vegetarian food by prior arrangement.

NUMBER 36 ♟

Howard Hotel, 36 Great King Street   031-557 3500

The Howard is looking to be the up-market discerning hotel in Edinburgh, in its sympathetically renovated Georgian New Town setting. The restaurant, in keeping with the hotel, is aiming high. This is modern British food in the professional chef vein, strong on technique and execution (there are a lot of juliennes and brunoises about to testify to the kitchen's aptitude with the knife), the main caveat might be that some dishes lack intent. To start, there's a good, fresh seafood 'brawn' filled with impeccable seafood with nicely varied texture and a tremendous saffron vinaigrette, but the accompanying quenelle of smoked trout although pleasant seems unrelated. Likewise a galantine of quail and rabbit on a base of crunchy caraway-flavoured pastry seems composed of individual elements which need uniting. Altogether faultless dishes include perfectly roasted rack of lamb flavoured with smoked garlic and a distinctly lamb flavoured 'jus' reduced to a perfect stage, served with a creamy potato gratin and fresh spinach. Sauces appear to be reliable with various elements balanced in harmony. Vegetarians are offered a clear first and main course option such as baked globe artichoke with a herbed crust, followed by filo-wrapped asparagus and pasta strudel with a creamy beurre blanc. Ingredients are above reproach, judgment, more or less reliable with the odd aberration like parsley sorbet. Wines are pricey, though there is a perfectly acceptable house wine on offer for under £10 to compensate. Lunch-time set menu represents good value. Delicious canapes such as hot smoked chicken rolls and tartare of salmon, or alcoholic coffee-time chocolates, make the end price seem acceptable. Service is highly experienced, friendly and knowledgeable, and given the setting, not at all stuffy.

Restaurant information

Getting there: Bus – 23/27
Landmark: Howard Hotel
Open: Seven days; 12.30–2.00p.m. and 7.30–10.00p.m. No lunch service on Saturdays.
Price per head (average): £14.75 (lunch) £27.50 (dinner); Diners, Access, Visa and American Express cards accepted.
Facilities: Children welcome; smoking in part.
Vegetarian food available

PARROTS ♙
5 Viewforth   031-229 3252

Squawk! If there is a medical term for obsession with parrots then it would be applicable to this eccentric neighbourhood bistro. Parrot pictures, parrot mobiles, parrot paper chains . . . the list is endless, integrated into a plush sub-Victorian decor in rich reds and brown with lots of velvet and busy carpeting. The management has seen fit to prohibit smoking totally not only within the restaurant, but also on the pavement outside (the fans draw in the fumes it claims). Quirkiness is not without appeal. Parrots is incredibly popular with a lot of repeat customers. Prices are keen, the menu (basic British with vegetarian leanings) is long, though the kitchen appears to be able to handle it. This must, in part, be due to the fact that the structures of the menu are samey, with certain key elements deployed variously in different assemblages. Most dishes come in starter or main course portions. There are competent meat satays, home-made soups, and reasonably accomplished vegetarian dishes like mung bean and cracked wheat biryani with an assertive gingery flavour and a savoury curry sauce, butter beans and vegetables au gratin, a respectable vegetable moussaka. Pies are in profusion – cottage, steak, game – with a small number of fish dishes. The kitchen and the clientele favour nursery puddings. Take your pick from spotted dick, bread and butter, treacle sponge, plum pudding, forest fruits sponge and more. There is also a good line in superior sorbets – peach, canteloupe melon, pineapple for example – bought-in, but French standard. Service is chatty, egalitarian, and male, full of personality and opinions. Music is jazz or nostalgia. Wines bear a resemblance to Oddbins round the corner and are for sale at bargain prices.

Restaurant information

Getting there: Bus – 11/16/17/23/45/47/71/C1/C11/C16/72/100/101/102

Open: Seven days; Sun–Thurs 5.30–10.30p.m. (last orders) Fri–Sat 12.30–4.00p.m. and 5.00–10.30p.m. (last orders). Throughout the Festival hours as Friday and Saturday.

Price per head (average): £6.00 (lunch) £7.50–£9.00 (dinner); all major credit cards accepted.

Facilities: Wheelchair access and disabled toilet; no smoking. Vegetarian food available

PIERRE VICTOIRE 🍴🍴

10 Victoria Street   031-225 1721 and 8 Union Street
031-557 8451

Pierre Levicky has given Edinburgh something which it badly
needed. First one, and now two, unfussy restaurants, where the
food is the thing and prices are kept low by compromising on frills,
not raw ingredients. The style is not conspicuously French and
studiously avoids the clichés of British 'French' food. This is never
a boring menu with uninteresting make weight options. You'll
find ingredients here (pigeon, oysters, guinea fowl, scallops) which
are more readily associated with up-market dining at more than
twice the price. Shellfish and fish are exceptional, invariably fresh
and served at prices which cause the odd stab of anxiety about the
establishment's ability to make a profit. There is nothing dull
about the approach either. There are classics such as sole in an
intense crayfish bisque-like sauce, but princess scallops are equally
well served with an orange and fresh coriander butter, or avocado
with fresh crab and a ginger vinaigrette. What's more, there is
variety in the saucing whether it's a light tomato and basil sauce to
accompany grilled halibut, or guinea fowl with sharp, clear lemon
juices, flavoured with tarragon. Desserts, which were once best
forgotten have been improved immeasurably and may include a
moist chocolate roulade, or curdy lemon tart. The wine list gets the
casual treatment with a lack of information about the producer,
but prices are very keen. Both restaurants fill up fast and regularly.
Noise and heat levels mount as the evening goes on as does the fog
of cigarette smoke. Quality control seems less acute in Victoria
Street, where the kitchen is more prone to taking licence when
under pressure. Sometimes this is endearing (when the chef decides
to abandon all but his boxer shorts), other times (when he forgets
to put the basil in the sauce or overcooks the vegetables), things
can become slapdash.

Restaurant information

Open: Mon–Sat; 12 noon–3.00p.m. and 6.00–11.00p.m.
(Sunday June–September and December)
Price per head (average): £4.90 (lunch) £11.00 (dinner); Access cards
accepted.
Facilities: Wheelchair access no disabled toilet, children welcome;
smoking throughout.
Vegetarian food available by prior arrangement

POMPADOUR ROOM ♟♟
Caledonian Hotel, Princes Street   031-225 2433

The Pompadour Room is an indulgence from start to finish. It has always had class, that splendid Grand Hotel feel, and the food has always been reliable. Nothing much has changed, the hotel around it has been upgraded to a 'Leading Hotel of the World', the Pomp sails on seemingly untouched. Since chef Alan Hill made his mark with it in the early Eighties, the style has always been nouvellish, albeit in the British Transport Hotel tradition, a mood continued by his successor Jeff Bland. Certain things can always be relied on. Your meat and fish will never be overcooked, the cheese board (flown in from Androuet in Paris and backed up by new wave Scottish cheese) is magnificent. The dessert trolley is decadent and shameless, with meticulous assemblages of chocolate, genoise, and impeccable tarts which actually taste as good as they look. Service is high-class and professional. There's a commitment to Scottish produce which shows up in dishes like the Pomp's own Musselburgh Pie (intense beef stew with mussels and paper-light puff pastry) which sometimes graces the lunch-time menu. But the tendency to paint pretty pictures on the plate, sometimes at the expense of taste is an ever-present ghost which needs exorcising. The set lunch menu is one of Edinburgh's great bargains. Mark-ups on wine are fierce. As we go to press a new chef is to be appointed, so style may change.

Restaurant information

Getting there: 3/4/9/15/31/44/10/16/33/26/11
Landmark: Caledonian Hotel
Open: Seven days; Mon–Fri for lunch. Mon–Fri 12.30–2.00p.m., Mon–Sat 7.30–10.30p.m., Sun 7.30–10.00p.m.
Price per head (average): £15.75 (lunch) £40.00 (dinner); all major credit cards accepted.
Facilities: Wheelchair access, disabled toilet; smoking in part.
Vegetarian food available

QUILLS RESTAURANT 🍴
Carlton Highland Hotel, North Bridge   031-556 7277

Despite the twee, contrived Victorian library decor, the atmosphere in Quills is warm, with a lot to recommend it. The clientele is that kind of world-weary, over-travelled business man, counting the days till he is back home in Adelaide, Tokyo or New York with his family. Quills à la carte and additional fish menus are vast (this is a busy hotel with a professional kitchen brigade), and there are enough similarities to lead to confusion when ordering. The classics are on the whole the best bet – seafood bisque and Provencal fish soup are both predicated on intense, crustacean flavoured fish stocks. Some modern dishes show flair along with an interest in things oriental, (wild duck breast in a rich brown sauce flavoured with five spice powder and ginger is a knockout). There is a tendency to absurd nouvellish garnishes which may include variously, nasturtium, strawberry, kiwi; and inevitably, the now ubiquitous bouquet of vegetables on the side accompanies. The cheese board features some of the best kept and most interesting French farmhouse cheeses to be found in the city; the Scottish representation is more hackneyed. The dessert trolley does its rounds but provokes little excitement. Impeccable front-of-house service of the kind that should win prizes.

Restaurant information

Getting there: Bus – 3/33/31/8/7/14/87
Landmark: Carlton Highland Hotel
Open: Mon–Sat for dinner, Mon–Fri for lunch; 6.30–10.30p.m. and 12 noon–2.30p.m.
Price per head (average): £15.00–£22.00 (lunch) £22.00 (dinner); all major credit cards accepted.
Facilities: Wheelchair access, disabled toilet; children welcome; smoking throughout.
Vegetarian food available.

THE RAJ 🍴

81–91a Henderson Street, Leith   031-553 3980

The Raj fits into the special effects camp of Indian restaurants. When it opened, its owner Tommy Miah had a live and massive elephant on site to make the point that the Raj had come to town. The restaurant is vast and airy in two definite sections, with the feel of a Somerset Maugham colonial bungalow. A cocktail bar, a collection of cane furniture and eclectic ornamental big cats and elephants, add a touch of Hollywood film set. Some may find this more appealing than the scene outside, which offers a realistic view through slatted wooden blinds into the seamy side of Leith-sur-mer. When it comes to eating, although the style is in a different league from the old 'International sauce'; this is successful formula food offering good value, which finds favour with the popular Scottish palate. Flavours are forceful and tasty in a one-dimensional way, though not necessarily over chilli-hot. Amongst the starters, essar bora (gram flour fritters with crushed prawn) are heavy, but well-spiced, with a colour which suggests art not nature. The chicken tikka is altogether better – moist inside, lightly seared with charcoal and flavoured with whole spices. Achar ghost, lamb marinated in pickle masala and flavoured with green chilli is a blockbuster dish which will wake up all but the most moribund taste buds. Blander dishes include Country Captain (described as a British army mess dish) of chicken and green peas flavoured with coriander or an appealing mushy vegetable Karrai. On the whole, the Raj offers less for vegetarians than its competitors do. The breads are not the lightest in the world. Basmati rice is nicely perfumed despite its lurid yellow appearance. The kitchen stretches to a pale green almondy kulfi ice-cream, but otherwise desserts are a standard, bought-in affair. Service is courteous, occasionally slow under pressure, and benevolent towards children.

Restaurant information

Landmark: Water of Leith
Open: Seven days; 12 noon–2.30p.m. and 5.30–11.30p.m.
Price per head (average): £5.95 (lunch) £12.50 (dinner); all credit cards accepted except Diners.
Facilities: Wheelchair access, disabled toilet; children welcome; smoking throughout
Vegetarian food available
Other services: Carry-out

RISTORANTE TINELLI 🍷🍷🍷
139 Easter Road   031-652 1932

Behind the modest facade of his restaurant within spitting distance
of the Hibs ground at Easter Road, Giancarlo Tinelli serves up the
best Italian food to be had in the city. The style is Northern, the
menu not large (about a dozen starters and fifteen main dishes),
but it is refreshingly different. Home-made air-dried beef (Bre-
saola) is magnificent, served in thin transparent slices with olive
oil, black pepper and parsley. Italian pork salami (Cotechino) is
served warm with well-flavoured lentils, quail roasted with
pancetta, veal cutlet pan-fried with a winey reduction flavoured
with sage and porcini mushrooms, and rabbit baked with a cream
and rosemary sauce. There's a proper risotto to be had or
home-made pasta – still a depressing rarity in a city with such a
large Italian population. Vegetables are limited, spinach, broccoli
and baby marrow, but each receives separate treatment. Salads are
unexciting. Desserts show better than most Italian establishments,
though they are clearly not the kitchen's main focus. There is
however, an interesting variation on crème brûlée where marsala
takes the place of caramelised sugar, and a volcanic looking Grand
Marnier-soaked sponge filled with ice-cream spills over with
vanilla custard and chocolate sauce. Tinelli's is unpretentious,
genuinely relaxed and relaxing. Service is slick and witty. Tremendous value for money.

Restaurant information

Getting there: Bus – 1/6
Open: Tues–Sat; 12 noon–2.30p.m. and 6.30–11.00p.m.
Price per head (average): £7.00–£9.00 (lunch) £12.00–£15.00 (din-
ner); Access and Visa cards accepted.
Facilities: Wheelchair access, no disabled toilet; children welcome;
smoking throughout.
Vegetarian food available

SCOTTISH NATIONAL GALLERY OF MODERN ART CAFE ♟

Belford Road   031-332 8600

The first thing that hits you when you walk into this gallery is the seductive smell of cheese scones and coffee that wafts up from the café below. No surprise then, that this café has a regular clientele whose motivation is more food than art. The café space is well-designed and aesthetic, offering the bonus of a paved patio with tables and a garden to sit outdoors in good weather. Hot dishes tend to be various – hot filo pastry roulades stuffed with well-flavoured meaty fillings, ostentatious pizzas and quiches, vegetable soups and substantial salads, the latter offering more interest than the standard array. The small selection of Scottish cheeses – some blues, some goats – are worth trying. Oatcakes and scones are reliable, as is the home-baking which majors on gooey slices of brownie, apricot flapjack and chocolate refrigerator cake. Pricing is fair, but you may end up paying more than you bargained for. Well-equipped for children with baby seats (in need of maintenance) and drinking beakers.

Restaurant information

Getting there: Bus – 13
Landmark: The Scottish National Gallery of Modern Art
Open: Seven days; Mon–Sat 10.30a.m.–4.30p.m. (lunch served 12 noon–2.30p.m.) Sun, light lunch available 2.00p.m.–4.30p.m.
Price per head (average): £5.00; no credit cards accepted.
Facilities: Wheelchair access, disabled toilet; children welcome; smoking permitted in part.
Vegetarian food available

SEEDS ♟
53 West Nicholson Street   031-667 8673

This is a tiny, some might say cramped wholefood restaurant run as a workers' co-operative. It would be easy to parody its right on-ness. The preoccupations of its patrons include shiatsu, eco-feminism, animal liberation and mountain bikes, (impossible not to get sucked into the conversations around you), but it would also be unfair. If basic surroundings (one wall of agit prop, uncomfy seats and oilskin table covers) bother you, it is worth remembering that Seeds has now served reliable vegetarian food for approaching ten years at ridiculously low prices. The menu is small and changes every day, cooked in the morning just in time to greet the lunch-time sitting. There is always soup – potato, onion and garlic is a favourite – and warm, moist brown bread to accompany and two hot dishes of the day. The repertoire for main dishes is quite wide and includes a warming wheatberry and vegetable stew or spinach lasagne, spilling over with vegetables and mushy lentils. This is an establishment which pays some attention to the seasons, and this shows in the salads which make the most of fleeting garden vegetables – rocket, landcress and lamb's lettuce – and fresh herbs, as and when available. Organic vegetables are used as much as possible and high quality ingredients like extra virgin olive oil are the order of the day. There is no reliance on the easy 'vegetarian' options of cabbage, beans and mayonnaise with everything. Puddings include a controversial tofu cheesecake which some love and others love to hate, and fresh fruit salad with velvety cashew nut cream.

Restaurant information

Getting there: 3/5/7/8/14/2/40/41/61/89
Landmark: Appleton Tower
Open: Mon–Sat; 10.00a.m.–8.00p.m.
Price per head (average): £2.00–£3.00; no credit cards accepted.
Facilities: Children welcome; no smoking
Vegetarian food available
Other services: Carry-out

SHAMIANA 🎭🎭🎭
14 Brougham Place   031-229 5578/228 2265

After more than a decade, the Shamiana still remains the benchmark against which good Indian restaurants of the meat-eating persuasion must be judged. Under the eye of its founding proprieter Moussa Joggee, now at the admirable Kalpna on the south side, it has set a standard for no compromise, authentic food which others have lacked the commitment to follow. The whole ethos is taste and judgment providing a showcase for complex and multi-faceted North Indian and Kashmiri cuisine. The restaurant is pleasing aesthetically – cool black and white tiling with mirrors which, like the food, has stood the test of time. Exquisite salt and sour Hyderabadi lamb with a lingering flavour of fennel seed shows the sophistication of which this kitchen is capable. Makhni choosa, spiced tandoori chicken in a buttery, rich spiced sauce puts similar offerings in other establishments in the shade. Vegetable cutlets come stuffed with comfortingly floury pulses and sprinklings of fresh spices which complement their creamy, piquant sauce. Once thought pricey, Shamiana's prices have held constant while others have risen.

Restaurant information

Getting there: Bus – 15/18/18A/24
Open: Seven days; lunch served Mon–Fri 12 noon–2.00p.m., dinner, Mon–Sun 6.00–11.30p.m.
Price per head (average): £8.00–£12.00 (lunch) £12.00–£25.00 (dinner); all major credit cards accepted.
Facilities: Wheelchair access, no disabled toilet; children welcome; smoking throughout.
Vegetarian food available
Other services: home catering for large parties by arrangement

SHORE 🏠
3 The Shore, Leith   031-553 5080

A cobbled street with seagulls squawking overhead forms the set for this popular bar-restaurant. There is more genuine continuity with the past here than some surrounding competition which rely on clichés to evoke Old Leith. Original dark wood and dull brass bar fittings and pearly lighting set the tone in the bar. In the restaurant area, white tablecloths, fresh flowers and nautical-ish stencils keep faith with the style but suggest a slower, more comfortable pace. This is good honest bistro cooking without pretension, a changing menu of eight starters and eight main courses, majoring heavily (and quite correctly in this setting) on fish. Soups are a strong point, with ingredients like celery and apple united with cream and a sound stock base to provide plenty texture and interest. Hot Arbroath smokie or herring on rye make good starters, as does black pudding fried and served with apple and mustard. Classic fish dishes are always on offer, like salmon with hollandaise, lemon sole with herb butter or trout Ardennaise, served in lavish portions with salad and vegetables. You may not want both – the salad is fresher than most with a decent coarse mustard vinaigrette, vegetables more interestingly cooked than is usual. Sliced potatoes may be oven roasted with lots of black pepper, courgettes quickly fried to successful caramelised effect. More elusive fish appear, like halibut and shark, and get less reverential treatment, steamed with leeks and ginger perhaps or with garlic butter and lemon. The kitchen makes technical faults

on occasion (fish either over- or under-done) but is happy to make amends if these are brought to its attention. The desserts are limited, ice-cream, cheesecake, apple pie *et al*. The Shore presents an interesting international portfolio of well-picked wines (some organic) and the prices are decidedly generous. Serving staff are by and large pony-tailed, colourful and trendy with an affable, egalitarian attitude. A full range of food is to be had in the bar, but smoke-sensitive souls may be asphixiated before it arrives. If ever there was a candidate for a no-smoking dining room, this is it.

Restaurant information

Getting there: Bus – 16/35/1/6/34
Landmark: Customs House
Open: Six days; Mon–Sat 11.00a.m.–midnight.
Price per head (average): £5.00–£8.00 (lunch) £8.00–£15.00 (dinner); no credit cards accepted.
Facilities: Wheelchair access, no disabled toilet; children welcome; smoking in part.
Vegetarian food available

SINGAPORE SLING 🍴
503 Lawnmarket (Royal Mile)   031-226 2826

Despite its location on the fringes of the Castle esplanade, this small Malaysian/Singaporean restaurant thankfully does not fit into the tourist trap bracket. The surroundings are modest (plastic pot plants, fairy lights and chiffon blinds) and with the exception of batik tablecloths, there is not a lot to suggest South-East Asia. Yet the kitchen manages to produce what has to be a strong contender for the best cuisine of its type in the city. Satay is a speciality and it tastes better than most: lightly seared on a charcoal grill leaving a lingering smoky flavour and served with a chilli dipping sauce topped with ground peanuts. Soups are light and appetising as witnessed by a light clear broth flavoured with sesame oil full of clear vermicelli, pickled vegetables and cucumber. The menu is helpful in indicating where a dish is predominantly Chinese or Malaysian/Singaporean. Both styles are effective. Steamed fresh fish of the day comes dressed with soy and fresh chilli with a topping of straw mushrooms, or vegetarian rice noodles, crunchy and aromatic with black beans, beansprouts and fresh greens. Rice tastes properly coconutty. Adventurous desserts like tropical palm pudding or red beans with agar agar, both served with coconut milk and palm sugar, add adventure. Very reasonably priced.

Restaurant information

Getting there: Bus – 1/6/34/35
Open: Seven days; lunch Mon–Sat 12 noon–2.00p.m., dinner Sun–Thurs 6.00–11.00p.m. Fri–Sat 6.00–midnight. The restaurant is open all afternoon during the summer.
Price per head (average): £4.50 (lunch) £6.90 (dinner); Access, Visa, American Express and Switch cards accepted.
Facilities: Wheelchair access, no disabled toilet; children welcome; smoking throughout.
Vegetarian food available

SKIPPERS BISTRO 🍴🍴
1a Dock Place, Leith   031-554 1018

You open the door from the cobbled street outside (thoroughly double-parked in true twentieth century fashion), into an old world. The atmosphere takes its lead from the decor, an old Leith bar well-worn and cluttered, a marble top bar, nautical maps and bric-à-brac, a lay-out which twists through nooks and crannies lending conviviality, and last but not least warmth; the sort of place where friends might have gathered on an inhospitable night. There the comparison with times gone by stops. There is no kitsch attempt to serve up an old Leith nostalgia package. Instead, there is the best sort of unpretentious real home-cooking, which knows its limits, and abides by them. The menu changes daily, not lock, stock and barrel, but dependent on what's fresh and good. Everything is as described, without attempts at artful embellishments. You might choose to start with potted crab, decently crabby and accompanied only by bread and salad or home-made fishcakes, full of discernible flakes of smoked haddock in a smooth potato mash, crisply fried and served with home-made tartare sauce. Those who crave complete simplicity can kick off with smoked salmon or gravadlax. Main courses, like starters concentrate on fish – of serious pedigree and quality. Monkfish tails are simply roasted and served with caramelised cloves of garlic, thick halibut steaks with a well-judged orange and stem ginger sauce, where the sweetness of the ginger is kept in check by the orange. The menu pays lip service to meat, takes no account of vegetarians. Side vegetables, however, which come as a standard accompaniment, such as leeks with cheese sauce, mangetouts and jacket potatoes, are less boring than in many establishments. Desserts, Tarte Tatin, white chocolate mousse, hazelnut cheesecake are reasonable, if uninspired in true home economics style.

Restaurant information

Getting there: Bus – 16/1/6/34/35
Landmark: Customs House
Open: Mon–Sat; 12.30–2.00p.m. and 7.30–10.00p.m.
Price per head (average): £12.50–£14.50 excluding wines; Access, Visa and American Express cards accepted.
Facilities: Wheelchair access, disabled toilet; children welcome; smoking throughout.
Vegetarian food available by prior arrangement.

SZECHUAN HOUSE 🮰🮰🮰
95 Gilmore Place   031-229 4655

The delicious aromas which curl out the kitchen window and perfume the pavement around offer the first sign to prospective diners that they are about to taste something special. Surroundings couldn't be more basic, as though someone had gone to the nearest Chinese supermarket and bought a flat-pack budget restaurant kit. Chinese character scrolls line the walls with typewritten translations underneath: 'Wherever you come from we are all brothers and sisters. This restaurant is full of good company' sets the restaurant mood. Chao-Gang Liu the chef, who is proud to tell us that he trained in the Hidden Hills Hotel, Kweilin, cooks authentic Szechuan food. The flavours are fascinating, hot, salt, sour, sweet and salty all at once, with plenty of spices and strong tastes. Soups should not be bypassed here. There is a thin, clear broth flavoured with Szechuan preserved vegetable (root of mustard green) with its deep earthy flavour and fresh Chinese cabbage with strips of pork. Or for those who want robust flavours, a terracotta coloured spicy soup, full of silky won ton enclosing tender minced pork tasting strongly of sesame oil and lots of fresh green chilli. The skill of the kitchen shows in dishes like the tea-smoked duck, where duck is first roasted to render its fat, then smoked over pungent black tea, then deep fried to crisp it up. Served with puffy, yeasty, shell-shape buns on the side, this is an incredible dish. Guai Wei chicken comes in shredded strips, sweet and moist and perfumed with musky fresh coriander. There's no shortage of interesting side dishes – salt and garlicky stir-fried green beans or crisp, deep-fried sweet potato. Aubergine is stir-fried with a slightly hot and sour sauce typical of the style of

this kitchen, where there are no uniform flavours but each mouthful offers variety and interest. For dessert, Szechuan sweet dumplings are glutinous and chewy – definitely an acquired taste – but the Szechuan pudding may find more support. This is a comforting mixture of fruit juice, rice flour and sugar which tastes a little bit like starchy caramelised apples. The prices are generously low, front-of-house service is charming and efficient, and children are given a warm welcome.

Restaurant information

Getting there: Bus – 9/10/27
Open: Tues–Sun; Sun–Thurs 6.30p.m.–midnight, Fri–Sat 5.30p.m.–3.00a.m.
Price per head (average): £8.10–£9.10; Visa and Access cards accepted.
Facilities: Wheelchair access; no disabled toilet; children welcome; smoking throughout.
Vegetarian food available.
Other services: Carry out

VERANDAH 🍴
17 Dalry Road   031-337 5828

The Verandah offers a basic and more or less reliable standard for sound, unflashy Indian food. On a good night, the food is subtle, aromatic and heartening. On off nights, tastes can merge and the same ingredients, (potatoes for example), can find their way into almost every dish. The decor relies on light cane and wood, and the food comes with a similar tone, innocent, on the whole, of artificial colourings. Tandoori dishes are competent standards, but some of the Verandah specials rise above that level. There is a rich tomatoey roghan josh, or methi ghust – tender lamb cooked with fenugreek and fragrant spices. Minced lamb with peas makes good comfort food, though sometimes it comes too well-anointed with ghee. Vegetarians do well here. The vegetarian thali (vegetables massallam, soupy dahl, warm chapati or roti and much more) is great value. The Verandah special ice-cream is a good, almondy kulfi. Always popular and more often than not, busy. Service on the desultory side, positively somnambulistic on occasion.

Restaurant information

Getting there: Bus – 4/44/3/33
Landmark: Haymarket Station
Open: Seven days; 12 noon–2.30p.m. and 5.00–11.45p.m.
Price per head (average): £9.95 (lunch) £11.95 (dinner); all major credit cards accepted.
Facilities: Wheelchair access, no disabled toilet; children welcome; smoking throughout.
Vegetarian food available
Other services: Carry-out

THE VINTNER'S ROOMS 🍴🍴
87 Giles Street, Leith   031-554 6767

It is hard to think of anywhere as hauntingly special as the beautifully proportioned and magnificently plastered seventeenth century Vintner's room in the historic Vaults at Leith. Tim and Sue Cumming have knocked down the sombre booths which lined the old bar, made singular into plural and extended the spirit of the room itself through the whole restaurant area. A huge fire dominates, candlelight alone illuminates. White napery and silver catch the eye. The menu offers a limited but realistic choice which will appeal to conservative diners escaping the faddishness of more 'modern' establishments. That is not to say that fashion is ignored – witness mango in place of melon as a partner to Parma ham – but old favourites like entrecôte sauce marchand du vin, are more at the heart of the cooking. Predictable offerings like smoked salmon with cucumber and dill rub shoulders with unusual dishes such as black soup of cuttlefish ink, with a good helping of crustaceans thrown in. Classics like skate in a browned butter sauce with capers are perfectly executed. There are good French provincial dishes such as a prune and almond tart flavoured with Armagnac. The cheese board offers more interest than most and is well-kept. The staff are obviously proud to work in such a special environment and show much enthusiasm – who can blame them?

Restaurant information

Getting there: Bus – 10/22/25/17/12
Open: Mon–Sat (Sundays on application and during the Festival); 12 noon–2.30p.m. and 7.00–10.30p.m. (longer during the Festival)
Price per head (average): £8.00–£11.00 (bar) £17.00–£23.00 (a là carte); Access, Visa and American Express cards accepted.
Facilities: Wheelchair access, disabled toilet; children welcome; smoking throughout.
Vegetarian food available
Other services: Carry-out if arranged in advance

VIVA MEXICO

10 Anchor Close, Cockburn Street   031-226 5145

Arguably the best of Edinburgh's Mexican restaurants, Viva Mexico has a loyal following for its filling hearty food. The atmosphere is jolly and youthful, and the food made up of permutations of refried beans, guacamole, soured cream, grated cheese and the standard Mexican-ish repertoire. High points are enchiladas and burritos or chilaquiles – tortilla chips, salsa, chicken, cheese and soured cream baked with copious amounts of chilli. There's a divinely starchy Mexican 'flan' for pudding if you feel in need of comfort food and the house does a mean Marguerita. Vegetarians have lots of choice. The food is cheap.

Restaurant information

Open: Seven days; Mon–Sat 12 noon–2.30p.m. and 6.30–10.30p.m. Sun 6.30–10.00p.m.
Price per head (average): £5.00 (lunch) £10.00 (dinner); Access, American Express and Visa cards accepted.
Facilities: Children welcome in the early evening; smoking throughout.
Vegetarian food available.

WATERFRONT WINE BAR 🍷
1c Dock Place   031-554 7427

The Waterfront is so popular that it is almost a victim of its own success. An atmospheric bar with conservatory attached, it is never short of customers, so the hassle involved in getting a table here has to be encountered to be believed. Lunch-times are less problematic – the management accepts reservations – but in the evenings, the pub ethos dominates and it is a free-for-all as to who can grab a table first. Smoking seems almost to be compulsory, and noise reverberates from hard surfaces. Once you have claimed a table the food ranges from staple wine bar fare – smoked mackerel pâté, garlic mushrooms, pickled herring (tasting home-made), estouffade de boeuf *et al* – to more interesting offerings which may include surf clams in the shell with a fishy tomato sauce, roasted rabbit with thyme, langoustine salads with home-made mayonnaise, trout with basil butter or for thorough-going vegetarians, a spinach and blue cheese pie in filo pastry. The prices are very reasonable, the plates loaded with food. Some might prefer fewer extraneous garnishes – dishes tend to come with a samey salad garnish which is less than inspiring, main courses with quantities of hot vegetables and potatoes in addition. Desserts eschew the easy bought-in catering options which turn up so frequently in wine bars. In their place, simple servings of goat cheese, or seasonal fruit such as cherries with a dollop of crème fraîche. There is a serious selection of wine by the bottle at very affordable prices, though the choice by the glass is more limited. Outdoor dining possibilities on the dock outside and under the comparative cover of the conservatory mark this out as a good place for summer eating, providing of course that everyone else in Edinburgh doesn't have the same idea.

Restaurant information

Getting there: Bus –16/1/6/34/35
Landmark: Customs House
Open: Seven days; Food served Mon–Thurs 12 noon–2.30p.m. and 6.00–9.30p.m., Fri–Sat 12 noon–3.00p.m. and 6.00–10.00p.m., Sun 12.30–3.00p.m.
Price per head (average): £7.60–£12.00; No credit cards accepted.
Facilities: Wheelchair access, disabled toilet; children welcome over five years old; smoking throughout.
Vegetarian food available

WHIGHAMS WINE CELLARS ♀
13 Hope Street, Charlotte Square   031-225 8674

An honourable wine bar of decent lineage, it is easy to walk by its unobtrusive basement entrance. Bags of historic New Town character, conspiratorial booths, aged stone walls, flagstone floor complete with sawdust. This is not, however, in the tradition which encourages its clientele to spit or sing sectarian songs, but rather to enjoy a well-chosen and fairly-priced selection of wines which incline to France. You eat here, less for the cooking (respectable soup, cauliflower cheese and so on) than the raw materials. Sparkling marine fresh oysters come from Loch Fyne as does the smoked salmon, both on offer at very competitive prices. Smoked venison also makes a regular appearance. With good brown bread and butter, nothing more is necessary.

Restaurant information

Getting there: All buses to the West end of Princes Street
Open: Mon–Sat; 11.00a.m.–midnight (Fri–1.00a.m.); lunch served 12 noon–2.30p.m. Food available in the evening during the Festival only.
Price per head (average): £6.00 (lunch); Visa cards accepted
Facilities: Children welcome; smoking throughout.
Vegetarian food available

WITCHERY ♟

Castlehill (Royal Mile)   031-225 5613

The Witchery has taken its eponymous theme and exploited it to the hilt. The decor is way over the top – sort of Vincent Price/Hammer Films set meets nursery school Hallowe'en. Low roofs and dusty crevices house real and artificially manufactured cobwebs, gnarled silver candlesticks provide the only light, and clients nudge the stuffed witch out of the way to sit upon the church-like pews. It isn't clear whether the management is parodying itself or acting in earnest, (those who value restraint may feel inclined to exit before scrutinising the menu), and misgivings may prevail in the presence of tartan cliches like Steak Balmoral and Old Mother Long Nose's Secret and Magic Mushrooms. Any grown-up who does persevere will be rewarded with food which tastes better than its stereotypical description, and shows evidence of good quality local ingredients. Starters include an unlikely smoked salmon and melon sorbet served with chilled melon (surprisingly refreshing and complementary), a large plateful of char-grilled langoustines (from Skye according to the menu) in a light garlic butter with lemon, or a warm scallop and mangetout salad on a bed of interesting salad leaves. Charcoal grilling lends interest to the many variations on steak, and classic dishes like poached salmon with hollandaise rub shoulders with baked monkfish tails with a creamy leek sauce, or duck served with a clove and heather honey sauce. For vegetarians, the kitchen runs to a charmingly rustic crunchy nut cutlet and not a lot else. Side vegetables are the usual predictable selection. For pudding there is a proper Scotch trifle, admirable prune and Armagnac-loaded ice-cream and more to toy with. Cafetière coffee is the order of the day. Curls of fresh unsalted butter show some care for details. Acceptable value for money, particularly in this touristy location. Keen value for lunch; serious wines at fair prices.

Restaurant information

Getting there: Bus – 1/6
Landmark: Edinburgh Castle
Open: Seven days; 12 noon–11.00p.m.
Price per head (average): £7.00–£9.50 (lunch) £17–£20.00 (dinner); American Express, Diners, Visa and Access cards accepted.
Facilities: Children welcome; smoking throughout.
Vegetarian food available

AMBER REGENT 🍴🍴
50 West Regent Street   041-331 1655

Behind its wonderful old red-brick facade, the Amber Regent looks and feels like a plush gentleman's club. You drop off your coat with the cloakroom mistress on the door and enter the inner sanctum, three rooms, one a bar. Even if you missed the brass plaque at the front door 'Authentic Cantonese Restaurant', you would realise instantly that this was not a run-of-the-mill Chinese eatery. The first thing that is different is the front-of-house staff, handsome youngish Chinese men sporting fashionably baggy suits, gorgeous women with sleek and actively trendy, angled bobs. The menu breaks the rules as well. No room is afforded to those ersatz dishes which habitually make up Scottish-Chinese menus. In its place, what the management assures us of is the real thing, not exclusively Cantonese but also Peking and Szechuan cooking. As you decide what to try – venison with mandarin sauce, seafood combination in bird's nest, Mongolian mushroom crispy rice soup to name but a few possibilities – you can observe that departure from the status quo has done nothing to deter trade. Behind the lacquer screens, you will see whole tableloads of business men tucking into their deep fried seaweed and crystal king prawn with abandon. Hot and sour soup is suitably hot and sour, conspicuously fresh scallops with their corals are steamed on the half shell and served with a pungently ginger and chilli dipping sauce. House specials, like mixed aubergine, mushroom and pepper stuffed with prawns and meat in a magnificent oyster sauce are grade A dishes. The kitchen is not above reproach, (aromatic crispy lamb was too fat and not at all crisp), but the general standard is still leaps and bounds ahead of most of the competition. The management has a sense of humour. Anyone fancy the 'Gang of Four' set dinner?

Restaurant information

Getting there: Underground – Hillhead
Landmark: Kelvingrove Art Gallery and Museum
Open: Seven days; Mon–Fri 12 noon–2.00p.m. and 5.00p.m.–11.30p.m., Sat 12 noon–midnight, Sun 5.00p.m.–11.30p.m.
Price per head (average): £4.50 (lunch) £10.00 (dinner); American Express, Diner, Visa and Access cards accepted.
Facilities: Smoking throughout

ASHOKA WEST END 🍴🍴
1284 Argyle Street   041-339 0936

The Ashoka is the antithesis of the cool colonial Indian restaurant school. There is a decadent feel, (some might characterise it as biliousness) enhanced by mock-Arabian carpets and greenish/ yellow ornamental glass. The musack is shamelessly loud and tasteless, spanning 'Bolero' and 'Don't cry for me Argentina'. None of this appears to be of any consequence to the teeming hordes of diners, who descend on it nightly for well-flavoured Indian food at very reasonable prices. The menu is vast and draws a distinction between the 'Gourmet's Choice' and the 'Popular menu', which suggests an identikit curry house approach. The food that emerges puts the lie to this with assertive but able spicing, distinctive flavours and the palpable freshness which shines out from busy kitchens. Basics like vegetable samosas are well-done in a crisp, ungreasy pastry with a tiny bowl of fresh coriander and root ginger spiked chickpeas on the side. Gujerati style dishes 'artfully prepared with yogurt and ground chana' are lemony sharp and creamy with discernible whole cumin seeds. A simple spinach and potato bhaji has its admirers, with a lovely slow-cooked taste and undertones of fresh and ground coriander. Dhall is hot, garlicky, gingery and comfortingly mushy. The kitchen knows when to leave well alone – no commercial mint sauce in the raita in this establishment. The nan is near perfect, crisp and flaky on the outside, yeasty and moist within. Irritations, apart from aural ones, include a sexist attitude amongst some otherwise friendly and vigilant table staff, who persist on directing all their attentions to men irrespective of who is ordering food or paying the bill.

Restaurant information

Getting there: Underground – Kelvinhall; Bus – 62/62B/64/64A/16/8/ 6/5/5A
Landmark: Kelvingrove Art Galleries and Museum, Kelvinhall Sports Centre
Open: Seven days; 5.00p.m.–12.30a.m.
Price per head (average): £7.00 (dinner); all major credit cards accepted.
Facilities: Children welcome; smoking throughout
Vegetarian food available
Other services: Home delivery and carry-out

BABBITY BOWSTER 🍴
18 Blackfriars Street   041-552 5055

This imaginatively designed bar and restaurant in the heart of the Merchant City is a favourite haunt of the Scottish literati, often the venue for poetry readings or similar events. Babbity's great strength is that it operates like a small hotel (there are six rooms in which you can stay over), so it offers a day-round service of food. Hearty cooked breakfasts start at 8.00 a.m. and thereafter food is served at the bar until 9.00 at night. Cooking is reliable, majoring in good Scottish produce like smoked salmon and Loch Etive mussels. Modern and traditional renditions of old Scottish favourites include potted hough on fingers of wholemeal toast, both meat and vegetarian haggis, and spiced chicken or lamb stovies, plus a meat pie – game, chicken or steak – depending on the mood of the kitchen. Changing daily specials (usually under £4) like minced lamb and oysters show imagination without contradicting the Babbity theme. Upstairs in the restaurant, you can spend more and dine more quietly though some may miss the conviviality of the bar below. Here the menu is more elaborate, (sole fillets stuffed with crayfish, venison with port and lemon), but in the same mood. Food is served outside on warm days.

Restaurant information

Getting there: Train – Queen Street
Landmark: Glasgow Cross
Open: Seven days; 8.00a.m.–midnight, Cafe Bar 12 noon–9.00p.m. Restaurant, 12 noon–11.30p.m.
Price per head (average): £3.50 (lunch); £7.50 (dinner); Visa, Access and American Express cards accepted.
Facilities: Wheelchair access; no disabled toilet; children welcome in restaurant and patio; smoking throughout.
Vegetarian food available

BABY GRAND 🍴
3–7 Elmbank Gardens   041-248 4942

Not easy to find, almost in the blue train station at Charing Cross, Baby Grand comes over like a flash, Manhattan-style diner. The cumulative effect of marquetry style wood, chrome trims, white table cloths and glass table tops is up-tempo New York. In the evening, to the tinkling strains of a very competent pianist, the atmosphere is deeply civilised and positively romantic. Food is cooked in full view, in the diner manner, which makes for occasional excitement with crackling flames from the charcoal grill. The end result is a good attempt at the up-market American deli tradition – grills (sirloin steak, lamb kebabs), sound sandwiches (pastrami, salt beef, croque monsieur) or simple favourites like bagels with cream cheese and smoked salmon. Much of this approach rests on ingredients. Scotland simply doesn't possess authentic pastrami for example, but the smoked salmon is infinitely superior to the greasy North American variety, so it's swings and roundabouts. An alien element – Spanish tapas – creeps in, to include a good home-made tortilla, fried sardines, Manchego cheese and chorizo sausage. There are desserts – cranachan, pecan pie, profiteroles, chocolate mousse – some made on the premises, others which represent the acceptable face of those bought in by restaurants throughout the city. Excellent cappuccino and espresso coffee. Service is flexible and pleasant, clientele well-behaved middle class professionals or the trendier business type. Some people who are less impressed by issues of decor and ambience may quibble about prices.

Restaurant information

Getting there: Train–Charing Cross Station
Landmark: Charing Cross Station
Open: Seven days; Mon–Thurs 8.00a.m.–midnight; Fri–Sat 8.00a.m.–1.00a.m., Sun 10.00a.m.–midnight
Price per head (average): £3.50 (breakfast) £5.50 (lunch) £8.00 (dinner); Access and Visa cards accepted.
Facilities: smoking throughout.
Vegetarian food available

BALBIR'S ASHOKA TANDOORI ♖
108 Elderslie Street   041-221 1761/2

Balbir's offers diners commercial Indian food, unsubtle perhaps, but with strong appeal, especially at the price. It is no exaggeration to say that three people could eat a massive banquet here and come home with change out of £30. Going by the 'bums on seats' principle, many Glaswegians are fully aware of this – Balbir's is invariably busy. Portions are large and seasonings forceful. Starters like the potato and gram flour fritters are solid and generously spiked with chilli. A good and very filling poori comes dry and ungreasy, though spoiled by its garnish of lurid chickpeas in a sweet, hot and vinegary sauce. (These chickpeas are a hallmark which Balbir's would be better without.) Main courses offer plenty of choice and span all the popular tandoori and curry dishes, but flavours are distinct with plenty of evidence of whole spices. For those who flavour milder dishes, a Ceylonese kurma with meat or vegetable makes an appealing option, with its pleasantly textured coconut-creamy sauce. House specialities like Punjabi massala – tender meat cooked with still discernible ginger, garlic, peppers and onions – is very savoury and moreish. All but the most degenerated tastebuds will wake up to the spicy-hot spinach paneer (actually tofu not curd cheese in this version). The nan bread is triumphant, marvellously seared with the smell of charcoal, light and yeasty inside. Standard desserts are relieved by a respectable selection of reasonable kulfis (Indian ice-cream) of which the mango is the best. Surroundings are comfortable, if badly lit, with wall murals of misty Himalayan peaks and subliminal piped Indian music. The staff are dead pan Glasgow, not without humour.

Restaurant information

Getting there: Train – Charing Crosss
Open: Seven days; 5.00p.m.–midnight
Price per head (average): £5.65 (lunch); £8.95 (dinner); all major credit cards accepted.
Facilities: Children welcome; smoking throughout.
Vegetarian food available
Other services: Limited home delivery service, 20 per cent discount on all carry-out food collected from restaurant.

BALBIR'S VEGETARIAN ASHOKA
141 Elderslie Street   041-248 4407

This is not the most sophisticated Indian vegetarian food in the world, but simple, basic cooking which provokes many warm recommendations from regulars. Portions are huge and prices are bargain basement so the Ashoka is always busy. There's an interesting range of Indian snacks, with the usual pakoras and samosas, crisp dosa masala (thin rice pancake stuffed with vegetables) or fiery lotus leaf rolls for those who like their flavours on the rough side. Devotees rave about the aloo tikki, a sort of spicy mashed potato roll. Main courses are voluminous, brimming bowls of over thirty variations on vegetables and pulses. Service is fast, friendly and intelligent with no bureaucratic obstacles if you choose, say, to have your starters at the same time as your main course. Children are especially welcome and get scaled down portions. Ashoka knocks a further 20 per cent off its already keen prices on takeaway, or in Glasgow speak, carry-out meals.

Restaurant information

Getting there: Train – Charing Cross
Open: Seven days; 12 noon–2.00p.m. and 5.00–11.00p.m., Sat and Sun 5.00p.m.–midnight.
Price per head (average): £5.50; all major credit cards accepted.
Facilities: Wheelchair access; no disabled toilet; children welcome; smoking in part.
Other services: Carry-out service available with 20 per cent discount on meals collected from restaurant.

BARBIZON RESTAURANT

Barbizon Gallery, 40 High Street   041-552 0707

This is a venue which points up the contradictions of the 'New Glasgow'. Inside, sympathetically restored gallery space, restaurant with larger than life Mackintosh-influence furniture and fashionable food. Outside, yuppie flats, not so distant high-rise blocks, a Miller Homes site in progress and Irn Bru cans caressed by the wind. This is the sort of place where, one suspects, the cooking varies according to who is on that day. Cooking has its highs and its lows. There are genuinely continental-tasting Toulouse and boudin sausages fried hard with terrific potatoes in their jackets and a curious, but successful 'ratatouille' with soupy brassicas in a vaguely curried tomato sauce. At under £4, this constitutes decent, honest bistro cooking. For lows, the dish of the day, herring fried in a mushy coating suggests porridge oats rather than oatmeal or otherwise reasonable crepes with good hot fruit, ruined by pink ice-cream. But it is a relaxing place to pass some time, the coffee is strong and ample and the restaurant is open throughout the day. Don't be in a hurry – service is affable but dozy.

Restaurant information

Getting there: Train – High Street
Landmark: Trongate clock
Open: Seven days; 9.00a.m.–midnight
Price per head (average): £5.00 (lunch); £8.00 (dinner); Access and Visa, cards accepted.
Facilities: Wheelchair access; disabled toilet; children welcome; smoking throughout.
Vegetarian food available
Other services: A collection from restaurant service is available.

BARCELONA ⌗

16 Byres Road   041-357 0994

It's easy to miss Barcelona's postage stamp front on the scruffy end of Byres Road with the merest flick of an eyelid and inside, though the ambience is cool, white and restful, the tables are definitely cheek by jowl. Tapas bars need to do two things to succeed – buy intelligently and cook well. A foray into the page-long menu yielded good results in the first category and mixed ones in the second. A platter of cheese offers generous slices of Manchego (Castilian cheddar), Idiazabal (shepherd's cheese from the Asturias) and Mahon (sweet Menorcan ewe's cheese) all in fine condition, fairly, indeed almost charitably priced at £2.95. Silver-soft, boneless boquerones (tiny sardines) are the real thing as encountered in Spain. Patatas bravas, spicy potatoes cooked with tomatoes, pungent paprika and a hint of chilli are comforting and more-ish, and a whole red pepper baked and stuffed with patently fresh hake is totally delicious. Other dishes are more hit or miss like the chicken cooked in oil and sherry vinegar which tastes too much of unreduced sherry. The biggest disappointment is Barcelona's rendition of that Catalan staple 'pan con tomate', where individual slices of toasted white bread should be rubbed with sweet, red tomatoes then drizzled with good olive oil and a liberal dusting of salt. Instead, large flat sheets of highly toasted bread on one side come spread with what tastes like tinned tomato pulp and no perceptible oil.

Overall a good attempt at authenticity which extends to an impressive Spanish wine list and Magno, that smart black Spanish soap in the washrooms. Very affordable.

Restaurant information

Getting there: Underground – Kelvinhall; Bus – 6/9/44/57
Landmark: Kelvingrove Art Galleries and Museum
Open: Tues–Sat; 12.00 noon–2.30p.m. and 7.00p.m.–midnight last orders 10.30p.m.
Price per head (average): £5.00 (lunch); £15.00–20.00 (dinner) including wine; Visa, Access and American Express cards accepted.
Facilities: Wheelchair access; no disabled toilet; children welcome at lunchtime; smoking throughout.
Vegetarian food available
Other services: Outside catering

BAR FAZZI 🍺
67 Cambridge Street   041-332 0941

This value-for-money cafe at the back of Glasgow's famed Italian delicatessen serves the gamut of pasta and changing daily specials including fantastic home-made Italian sausages spiced up with chilli and fennel seeds served with peas and potatoes, or putanesco and deliciosa pasta sauces amongst others. Liqueur-soaked sponges are not to be missed and the Tiramisu, a rich concoction of mascarpone cheese with coffee and spirit-laden sponge is heaven. Fazzi's own roasted coffee produces truly marvellous espresso and cappuccino coffee. Small, invariably busy and popular with chain-smokers, so it seems. Eat cheaply and well here then blow a tenner in the shop.

Restaurant information

Getting there: Underground – Cowcaddens
Landmark: Hospitality Inn
Open: Seven days; 8.00a.m.–10.30p.m.
Price per head (average): £6.00; Access and Visa credit cards accepted.
Facilities: Wheelchair access and disabled toilet; children welcome; smoking throughout.
Vegetarian food available

BASIL'S 🍴
184 Dumbarton Road   041-337 1416

Basil's clientele is afforded more comfort and leg room than is usual in earnest veggie establishments. Decor is positively stylish – slatted blinds, smart lighting and Mackintosh wood-framed mirrors. A similarly light touch prevails with the food. Out with that leaden brown wholemeal pastry and in with a crisp variety. Vegetarian cliches like baked potatoes rub shoulders with a smoky leek and tofu cocktail. Cracked wheat and vegetable roast takes the place of the standard nut one. Salads are crunchy and athletic. The bread, all baked on the premises, is compulsive and can make a meal along with say, the cider and onion soup. The kitchen is big on Greek yogurt, right down to a fruits of the forest brûlée, where the yogurt replaces cream. Chocolate cheesecake beckons to those determined to indulge. All this is proof that to stick to vegetarian/ humanistic principles, you don't have to wear Pictish woad. For despite signs of outward decadence, Basil's is firmly a workers' co-operative, committed to source ingredients produced without animal or human exploitation or environmental destruction. No danger of bumping into Cape fruit or Nestlé milk here. Instead there's Frontline tea, Campaign coffee and organic wines. The philosophy is very definitely bread and roses.

Restaurant information

Getting there: Underground – Kelvinhall; Bus – 64/62/62A
Landmark: Bottom of Byres Road
Open: Seven days; 12 noon–9.30p.m.
Price per head (average): £8.00 (lunch) £10.00 (dinner); No credit cards accepted.
Facilities: Wheelchair access and disabled toilet; children welcome; smoking in part only.
Vegetarian food available

THE BUTTERY 🍺🍺
652 Argyle Street   041-221 8188

The setting for the Buttery would go down well in a surrealist, art house movie. It is another of Glasgow's food institutions, behind an unlikely facade in the last tenement left in the middle of a gap site. Once inside. the atmosphere is heavily Victorian, dark, discreet and almost conspiratorial. If you can't find a media, political or business face in here then you simply haven't been reading your newspapers. Under the influence of its now departed chef Brian Graham, the Buttery specialised in a few classic dishes interspersed with bold and eclectic combinations (some of which worked, others which didn't) – a tradition which seems to be continued by his successors. Classics like carré of lamb with its kidneys and Madeira, and salmon with red wine sauce rub shoulders with unlikely modern dishes such as turkey and chestnut ravioli with green peppercorn sauce and beef with beansprouts and a caramelised garlic sauce. Desserts continue to be predictable: crême brûlée, meringue, ice-cream and sorbets, but well-executed.

Restaurant information

Getting there: Train – Anderston Station
Open: Mon–Sat; Mon–Fri 12 noon–2.30p.m. and 7.00–10.00p.m., Sat 7.00–10.00p.m.
Price per head (average): £25–30.00 (lunch) £30–37.00 (dinner); American Express, Diners, Visa and Access cards accepted.
Facilities: Wheelchair access; no disabled toilet; children welcome; smoking throughout.
Vegetarian food available

CAFE GANDOLFI ☙
64 Albion Street   041-552 6813

However you feel about the changing face of the Merchant City, you have to admit that Cafe Gandolfi tops the style stakes. It is Glasgow's original, design-conscious eating place, and has yet to be bettered for genuine, as opposed to contrived, atmosphere which is both civilised and cosmopolitan. The magnificent exaggerated marquetry effects of Tim Stead's furniture have stood the test of time and only get better. High ceilings, tongue and groove panelling and additions like the electric blue stained glass 'flock of fishes' – the deserved winner of a Saltire award – round off the effect. The food is not as exceptional as the environment, though reliable for the most part with the odd touch of flair. Breakfasts are a strong point starting with a pick-me-up of whisked bananas, yogurt and honey, followed by oeufs en cocotte and potent espresso coffee. Throughout the day, there is an interesting selection of flexible brasserie food which might comprise foreign favourites such as grilled red peppers in opulent extra virgin olive oil, a well-rendered salade Niçoise, or patriotic dishes like Finnan haddie with potatoes, gravadlax and smoked venison. Ingredients are fresh and discriminatingly chosen, showing good taste. No naff touches like commercial thousand island or cucumber relish here. The little chocolate pots are just the thing to toy with while glancing around the fascinating collection of black and white Glasgow café photos with Scott Joplin playing unobtrusively in the background. Wines from La Vieille Ferme brighten up an otherwise lack-lustre selection.

Restaurant information

Getting there: Train – High Street; Underground – Buchanan Street;
Landmark: The City Halls
Open: Seven days; 9.00a.m.–11.30p.m.
Price per head (average): £3.00 (breakfast) £10.00 (lunch & dinner); no credit cards accepted.
Facilities: Wheelchair access; no disabled toilet; children welcome; smoking throughout.
Vegetarian food available

CAFFE QUI AND CANTINETTA ⌂
17 John Street   041-552 6099/4842

This aesthetic concoction of marble, wrought iron and exaggerated chandeliers in the upwardly mobile Merchant City feels very Italianate, so it comes as something of a surprise to find out that it is owned by Scottish and Newcastle Breweries. Obviously our brewers have improved their taste when it comes to commissioning architects. But having the nous and commercial sense to have a site designed with panache is one thing, getting the food right is another. Style minus content is the current Glasgow food disease – a pitfall which Qui happily transcends. Grill-toasted focaccia from Glasgow's own Fratelli Fazzi come filled with melted mozzarella, and better-than-average tomatoes. Okay, the basil that is sprinkled on is dried, not fresh, but you can't complain because they are cheap. Fresh pizzas, baked on the premises taste and smell good, though not authentically Italian and you may have to choose astutely to avoid more disappointing dishes. Liqueur-soaked Italian desserts are imported from Italy – Tiramisu, Amaretto sponge and Torta di Qui – a formidable combination of cream cheese and raisins steeped in rum, with a layer of chocolate and hazelnuts. An airy conservatory offers the opportunity to oversee the perpetual building works in progress. A complete cross-section of the day's press and the aroma of strong espresso coffee make this a congenial place in which to while the hours away. Down below, there is a gloomy basement restaurant which feels in need of an identity, so stay above ground.

Restaurant information

Getting there: Underground – Buchanan Street
Landmark: George Square
Open: Seven days; Mon–Thurs 8.30a.m.–7.30p.m., Fri 8.30a.m.–6.30p.m., Sat 9.30a.m.–6.30p.m., Sun 12.30–7.30p.m.
Price per head (average): £1.30–£8.00; Mastercard, Visa, Access and Diners cards all accepted.
Facilities: Wheelchair access; no disabled toilet; children welcome; smoking in part food only.
Vegetarian food available.

CITY MERCHANT 🍴🍴
97 Candleriggs   041-553 1577

The City Merchant is one of those restaurants with genuine atmosphere, the kind that arises naturally when staff are amiable, customers happy. It is hard to put your finger on exactly why it works, the internal dynamics of the room perhaps with its original dark-stained wood, and busy Edwardian atmosphere. This is an establishment which works like clockwork under the ever vigilant eye of its proprieters, with strong appeal to all kinds of people. One of the few places where family groups, new Glaswegians and business types are to be found side by side. Food has to be part of it, an ambitiously large menu (three in fact, the regular one, set lunch and blackboard-posted daily specials), which courts disaster with an eclectic Scottish-Italian-French selection. The results are always reasonable (a blandish smoked salmon soup pepped up with fresh salmon quenelles) on occasion sensational (formidable fresh ravioli stuffed with ricotta and spinach with a knock-out fresh vegetable and fines herbes sauce seductively reeking of fresh tarragon). Fresh fish is to be had in profusion, and there is no doubting the quality and standard of ingredients which pass through the kitchen, as witnessed by expertly moist monkfish in a rich langoustine sauce. Vegetarians will not be at a loss with good pastas, bean and vegetable concoctions. There is plenty evidence of fresh herbs, good salad leaves and selective buying – moist smoked duck and goose breast, for example. You could spend a lot of money here if you go for lobster, duck or steak. Less protein-intensive eating will produce much more modest accounts. The kitchen apparently runs out of steam by dessert time – puddings are profoundly ordinary.

Restaurant information

Getting there: Train – High Street; Bus – Trongate/High St/George St
Landmark: The City Halls and Ticket Centre
Open: Mon–Sat; Mon–Fri 12 noon–2.30p.m. and 5.00–11.00p.m., Sat 9.00a.m.–11.00p.m.
Price per head (average): £4.95–£15.00 (lunch) £6.50 (pre theatre) £18.50 (dinner); Access, Visa and American Express cards accepted.
Facilities: Wheelchair access; disabled toilet; children welcome; smoking throughout.
Vegetarian food available

CUL DE SAC CREPERIE
44–46 Ashton Lane   041-334 4749

Low ceilings and cottagey windows give this atmospheric crêperie an almost Toytown feel. Despite its period opalescent lights and leaded glass, the whole place generates happy-go-lucky youth with a view into the kitchen to catch the chef's banter. Smells of sizzling crêpes evoke the Eiffel Tower and the reality is no disappointment. Crisp, dry and deliciously light buckwheat crepes come stuffed with a selective choice of fillings, of which the spinach and cheese is most effective. Home-made burgers (made with 100 per cent steak mince the menu tells us) constitute great value and in common with side salads and chips, come in two sizes to suit varied appetites. Discriminating burger toppings (cheese, au poivre, chilli) are on offer as extras. Plats de jours include fresh langoustine with pernod or classics like beef chasseur. Go for the sweet crêpes for pudding. There's a better-than-average wine list at reasonable prices, an international representation of beers, and Babycham or Bollinger to cater for all Glasgow tastes.

Restaurant information

Getting there: Underground – Hillhead
Landmark: Glasgow University
Open: Seven days; Mon–Thurs 5.00–11.30p.m., Fri–Sat 12 noon–midnight, Sun 12 noon–11.00p.m.
Price per head (average): £8.00–£12.00 (lunch) £12.00–£15.00 (dinner); American Express, Diners, Visa and Access cards accepted.
Facilities: Children welcome; smoking throughout
Vegetarian food available

d'ARCY'S 🍴🍴

Basement Courtyard, Princes Square   041-226 4309

d'Arcy's has a great buzz, granite table tops and actively trendy furniture. The menu is large, interestingly varied and portions are huge. You can have an excellent salade niçoise, spilling over with grade one olives and anchovies with the unmistakable flavour of top-quality extra virgin olive oil, an aromatic stir-fry or a platter of well-chosen and kept Scottish, Irish and English farmhouse cheeses. There are signs of a pâtisserie fanatic in the kitchen where the German pastry chef whisks up moist hazelnut and chocolate cakes and cherry and apple tortes to continental standards, before serving them in a gloriously vanilla-flavoured crème anglaise. Over the way you'll find d'Arcy's 'Comestibles and Bespoke Sandwich Shop'. Despite its cute little title, it succeeds in offering a staggering array of sandwiches with everything from rare roast beef to pan yan pickle. You can phone or fax your order by 10.30 a.m. (Fax: 041 221 5869) and they guarantee delivery by 12 noon.

Restaurant information

Getting there: Underground – Buchanan Street
Landmark: Princes Square
Open: Seven days; Mon–Sat 12 noon–10.00p.m.; Sun 12 noon–4.00p.m.
Price per head (average): £12.00 (lunch) £15.00 (dinner); all major credit cards accepted.
Facilities: Smoking throughout.
Vegetarian food available

DI MAGGIO'S 🍴
61 Ruthven Lane   041-334 6000

Not the easiest restaurant to find, stuck up at the muddy and unpromising looking end of Ruthven Lane. (The painless way to avoid the trail is to walk up Ruthven Street then turn left.) This thriving pizza and pasta place exudes the delicious aromas of garlic and espresso coffee. As the day goes on, so the place fills up, with a youngish clientele who like the beer, the buzz, the Chianti bottles with dripping candles and the black and white nostalgia pictures of Jimmy Dean and Marilyn. Di Maggio's pizzas, made on the spot, are thin and crisp with twenty toppings to choose from : four cheese (melting and substantial), piccante (with spicy Italian sausage) and much more. Indecisive souls can opt for one pizza with two different toppings if they like. Standard pastas like fusilli with cream, ham, peppers and peas are rendered crudely, but acceptably, composite dishes such as cannelloni gratinata, with its moist stuffing of spinach and ricotta in a very respectable cheese sauce, are much better than average. Side dishes include straightforward deep-fried mozzarella with a well-made tomato sauce and there are good burgers with selective toppings – Swiss cheese, au poivre, piccante. Desserts are unexciting, coffee invigorating. Very affordable.

Restaurant information

Getting there: Underground – Hillhead
Open: Seven days; 12 noon–2.30p.m. and 5.00p.m.–midnight
Price per head (average): £3.00 (lunch) £9.00 (dinner); Access and Visa cards accepted.
Facilities: Children welcome; smoking throughout.
Vegetarian food available
Other services: Home delivery and carry-out

FIRE STATION 🍴
33 Ingram Street   041-552 2929

The title is not a gimmick (even if some of the food is) – this is indeed an old converted fire station, built in a lavish and opulent style. Elaborate marble lines the walls, and any echoing sarcophagus effect is diminished by a tier of raised tables set around them, with more tables on what feels like the sunken area inside. So cavernous is this building, that it can seem quiet even when relatively busy, almost eerie at off-peak. There is a partially open kitchen with serious-looking chefs in whites behind. They cook from an eccentric but enthusiastic menu. You may not agree with the management that deep-fried ravioli is about to become one of the most popular dishes in Britain, but the results are not inedible. Aberrations apart, the cooking is for the most part quite reasonable. Pastas (Milanese, smoked salmon farfalle, seafood fusilli) form the core with more than a casual nod towards vegetarians. They choose extensively from dishes like summer spaghetti with a sharp. yogurty sauce, wholemeal pasta with garlicky vegetables, baked vegetables with cream and emmenthal. Some work, others are problematic – the stir-fry is a wok-full of interesting vegetables too coarsely cut and only partially fried – but most attempts are good and honest with fresh ingredients the obvious raw material. Salads, (curly lettuce, sliced tomato *et al*) need upgrading. For pud, pancakes and strudels or good old Anton's bread and butter pudding – not quite up to the eponymous chef's standard, but an honourable effort. Service pouts, gyrates to music and chatters to customers – fun if you like that sort of thing. The set lunch menu is a bargain.

Restaurant information

Getting there: Underground – Buchanan St
Open: Seven days; Mon–Thur 12 noon–2.30p.m. and 5.00–11.30p.m. Fri 12 noon–2.30p.m. 5.00–12.30a.m. Sat 12 noon–1.00a.m. Sun 12 noon–11.30p.m.
Price per head (average): One course lunch Mon–Sat £2.55, Sun brunch £3.95, Sun–Thurs 5.00p.m.–7.00p.m. half price pasta; Visa and Access cards accepted.
Facilities: Wheelchair access and disabled toilet; children welcome; smoking throughout.
Vegetarian food available

FREED'S ♟

49 Copelaw Street   041-423 8911

Hidden away inside the Jewish Welfare Board centre, you'll find this utilitarian restaurant which may strike senior citizens as reminiscent of a wartime 'British Restaurant' complete with Sixties conversions – echoing walls, plastic chairs and fake teak. Only the aged posters of Elat and Jerusalem, and the Klezmer music in the background point to any sort of cultural identity. In the Nineties, it might make the perfect set for a Channel Four play, but more to the point, it offers access to traditional Jewish home-cooking, produced by Mr Freed in person, with the sanction of the Glasgow Beth Din. Eating here is charitably priced – it is possible to enjoy a filling meal for a couple of pounds – and it is the kind of cooking which would restore your flagging spirits after getting drenched in the rain. This is comfort food par excellence. You start off with good, moist rye bread loaded with caraway seeds (no butter of course) and take your pick from starters like chopped liver, hummus or warming chicken soup with lockshen noodles or kneidle bread dumplings. This kitchen has frying down to a tee, with basics like fish and chips to perfect potato latkes (crisp on outside, moist within) or chopped fried fish cakes – light and airy with a crunchy matzo meal exterior. Beetrooty horseradish complements the fried dishes, but there's bad old HP or tomato sauce if you prefer. Pudding fans are advised to head for the lockshen pudding, a glorious assembly of caramelised noodles and dried fruit, loaded with cinnamon. Coffee is instant and there is no mineral water. The waitresses are welcoming, happy to explain what's what, and positively kindly. A regular clientele with a good neighbourly atmosphere.

Restaurant information

Open: Sun–Thur; 12.30p.m.–2.30p.m. and 5.30p.m.–8p.m.
Price per head (average): £3.00 (lunch) £6.00 (dinner); no credit cards accepted.
Facilities: Smoking throughout; unlicensed.

GOURMET HOUSE 🍴🍴
19 Ashton Lane   041-334 3229

Another good food option in the bustle of well-endowed Ashton Lane, there's more to Gourmet House than the standard Scottish Cantonese dishes. In amongst the standard repertoire you will find special interest in Szechuan dishes like crunchy beef fillet with sesame seeds and preserved vegetables or a fascinating vegetarian soup, full of seaweed, beancurd, Chinese black fungus and more. The biggest excitement is that unlike many of its compatriots, Gourmet House makes efforts to serve its fish without first introducing it to the deep freeze, hence the daily seafood menu, where you can choose fresh Scottish lobster, scallops, squid, crab and Dover sole straight from the Ayrshire coast, lightly steamed and seasoned in the best Chinese fashion. A whole steamed Dover sole will cost you £8.50, but it is well worth it for this fine fish so deliciously cooked and deftly removed from irritating bones. Other Gourmet House specials show that the kitchen staff are no lowly wielders of woks, but highly skilled: try the crisply grilled breast of duck with its king prawn forcemeat and crab sauce for evidence of that. A plush, red, pagoda-like atmosphere sets the tone in this well-maintained restaurant. Staff, both Scottish and Chinese, are really friendly and children are given VIP treatment.

Restaurant information

Getting there: Underground – Hillhead
Landmark: Kelvingrove Art Gallery and Museum
Open: Seven days; Mon–Sat 12 noon–2.00p.m. and 5.00p.m.–midnight
Price per head (average): £5.00 (lunch) £10.00 (dinner); American Express, Diners, Access and Visa cards accepted.
Vegetarian food available

THE GRANARY ♟

82 Howard Street   041-226 3770

Anyone who wants to escape the relentless pace of twentieth century consumerism in the St Enoch centre can make a bid for freedom out the back door to this curiously anachronistic wholefood restaurant. The atmosphere is Miss Marple Village Tea Shoppe, complete with tiered cake racks, fluted glass cake stands and comforting antique furniture. The food is far from whimsical. This is mainstream vegetarian cooking without hessian tendencies. Hot dishes like walnut and cheeseburgers taste like they sound, any boredom offset by a lively home-made tomato sauce. Staple soups like lentil are warming, the ubiquitous quiche appears in a more interesting form as a French onion tart, and you are spared the customary layer of soggy pastry below. In fact, pastry is a strong point throughout, crisply cooked, crumbly and short, either in a savoury form, or in fresh rhubarb or apple tarts. For those who wince at the sight of bowls of salads, the Granary's selection is fresher and more generous than usual. Baking is hardly healthy: fantastic nutty meringues, tooth-rottingly sweet ginger toffee fudge and crisp brown empire biscuits which lure to you destruction like a siren on the rocks. There's bread, cakes and nearly anything served on the premises to take away. Excellent value for money.

Restaurant information

Getting there: Underground – St Enoch Centre
Landmark: Behind St Enoch Centre
Open: Mon–Sat; 8.30a.m.–6.00p.m.
Price per head (average): £3.50; no credit cards accepted.
Facilities: Wheelchair access; disabled toilet; children welcome; smoking in part
Vegetarian food available
Other facilities: Carry-out.

GROSVENOR CAFE
35 Ashton Lane   041-357 3286

Included in this guide, not by virtue of its food but for its atmosphere. This is the archetypal Scottish-Italian cafe, which has to strike a note with anyone who grew up in the Fifties or Sixties. The formula proves so popular that there is a perpetual queue at the door. Low beams, plastic bench seats and busy vinyl wallpaper and plastic Sixties light shades vie with a high shelfed knick-knack collection of wooden animals, old tea tins, Thirties flower bowls. This is the sort of place where the waitresses plonk a tumbler of hot tea with the tea bag still in it down in front of you with a 'there you go' or a 'cheery bye' to the last customer. It is impossible to spend any serious amount of money here. The food is ultra-basic : fried egg rolls, croissants with peanut butter or nutella, half a pizza with an egg on top – most of which return significant change of a pound. The clientele is Tutti-Frutti like – spotty boy students downing hamburger rolls, caramel wafers and Irn-Bru, wee old lady shoppers with grandchildren, or style-conscious youth pretending to be James Dean. Upstairs, a more expensive but still ludicrously cheap restaurant serves upgraded food in the same cafe tradition but the atmosphere can't match below.

Restaurant information

Getting Underground: Underground – Hillhead
Landmark: Glasgow University
Open: Mon–Sat; 12 noon–3.00p.m. and 5.00–8.00p.m.
Price per head (average): £4.00 (lunch) £11.00 (dinner); no credit cards accepted.
Facilities: Children welcome; smoking throughout.
Vegetarian food available

THE HORSESHOE BAR
17–21 Drury Street 041-221 3051

A curiosity frozen in time, the Horseshoe Bar encapsulates the best features of a traditional Scottish pub. You will find it listed in the Guinness Book of Records as having the longest bar in any pub, (all 104 feet and 3 inches of it to be precise). Deservedly, it is something of a Glasgow institution: offering a glimpse of a real cross-section of pre-Miles Better Glasgow life. An elaborate polished wood bar, Art Nouveau tiles, and stained glass barely changed since the place was built, play on the horseshoe theme. The pub hosts scores of bunneted old men, lady shoppers and impoverished students of the untrendy variety. Somehow, although a woman can comfortably drink on her own in the bar downstairs without wayward glances or hassle, the sexual divide lives on as most women gravitate to the lounge upstairs. Waitresses serve school dinner food at a cracking pace, offering a formula three course meal for a bargain basement price. Plates are heaving with steak and kidney pie, macaroni cheese, cold meat salads with hot vegetables and chips, nursery rice pudding and wobbly pink jelly. Love the food or hate it, the experience is not to be missed.

Restaurant information

Getting there: Underground – Buchannan Street
Landmark: Central station
Open: Mon–Sat; 12 noon–8.00p.m.
Price per head (average): £.60 (lunch) £1.00–£6.00 (dinner); no credit cards accepted
Facilities: Children welcome; smoking throughout.

JANSSEN'S 🍴
1355 Argyle Street   041-334 9682

Down town Amsterdam comes to Glasgow in the form of this brasserie with an authentic European feel, run by a Dutch proprietor. A large wrought iron candelabrum dominates, and Thirties lights and black rubber table mats make a design-conscious statement, though some may yearn for more softness and comfort. The menu is varied and interesting with Indonesian influenced dishes such as grilled marinated pork served with a peanut satay sauce or chargrilled merguez sausages. After lunch and before dinner savoury food, (tzaziki, chorizo with marinated olives, roasted almonds with cured ham) is on offer in intelligent tapas-size portions. There are some interesting though simple desserts – baked bananas in rum, marinated prunes, Dutch appelbol, amaretto and raspberry cream. Janssen's operates on the laudable European principle of flexible dining, which can cope with one person at the table wanting only a coffee while the others want a full meal. This is the kind of brasserie which goes beyond the smoky Scottish pub with food, to create a civilised licensed environment where children are genuinely accommodated and adults can enjoy a drink. Regulars, a mixture of academics, nurses and doctors and West Enders, come to pretend that they are back on holiday again. Prices are keen and there are good touches like walnut vinaigrette to add interest to otherwise standard salads. Very popular so booking in the evening is recommended. An attractive retreat at the end of a long hard trip around Kelvingrove Art Galleries opposite. There's a decadent champagne brunch on Sundays.

Restaurant information

Getting there: Underground – Kelvin hall; Bus – 57/59.
Landmark: Kelvingrove Art Galleries and Museum
Open: Seven days; 11.00a.m.–11.00p.m.
Price per head (average): £4.50 (lunch) £10.00 (dinner); Access and Visa cards accepted.
Facilities: Wheelchair access, disabled toilet; children welcome; smoking throughout.
Vegetarian food available

JIMMY'S ♟

1 Victoria Road   041-423 4820

Un-believers who would see fit to question the dogma that there's no beating British (and particularly Scottish) fish and chips could be persuaded to reassess after a trip to Jimmy's. Sprawling premises on the relentless Eglinton Toll transection are part bar, part restaurant. Viewed on a wet Glasgow day, it looks unpromising and inside, though efforts have been made to create a marine effect (the decor is suitable ocean blue, leaded glass fish panels and fish shaped blackboards), there is a touch of plasticity which makes you wonder if you are being manipulated. Misgivings evaporate when food arrives – fish and chips of such perfection that it invites poetry. Start with the fish, haddock, sole, salmon, plaice sent down from Peterhead or Aberdeen that morning, with a palpably fresh marine flavour. Then the batter, so light-crisp and accomplished that it rustles like taffeta, and remains in this state as you eat it – no subcutaneous layer of stodgy batter here. Next the cooking oil, always groundnut, which makes for crunchy exterior chips with a soft squashy centre which taste utterly home-made, a fact that is underlined by their rugged and irregular sizes. It is no exaggeration to say that Jimmy's excellence exposes the tired haddock (often whiting pretending to be haddock) in soggy batter with greasy lard-fried chips which commonly passes for this favourite national dish. The biggest revelation is the salmon, moist and succulent once batter fried by this method – forget the steaming, hollandaise and prissy saucing, this is the way to eat it! The service is fast and friendly. Children are positively welcomed and comfortably accommodated in state of the art high chairs. An international array of beers is more in keeping with the malt vinegar and tomato sauce than the wine.

Restaurant information

Getting there: Train – Bridge Street
Landmark: Eglinton Toll
Open: Seven days; Mon–Fri 11.00a.m.–3.00p.m. and 5.00–11.00p.m., Sat–Sun 11.00a.m.–11.00p.m.
Price per head (average): £3.75 (lunch) £5.00–£6.00 (dinner); Access, Visa and Style cards accepted
Facilities: Wheelchair access, disabled toilet; children welcome; smoking throughout.
Vegetarian food available
Other services: Carry-out

JOHN STREET JAM
John Street   041-552 3801

When you walk into this cavernous building, you have a choice. Hang out downstairs with a mass of chattering students, who come primarily to drink, (although there are basics snacks to be had) or scale the dizzy heights of the balcony floor where a slightly sunken raft offers the potential for more civilised dining. The jazz is loud, the menu American with Cajun specialities. Since alligator tails are never what you might call in season here, the finger has to point to the deep freeze. Nevertheless, the blackened cajun chicken is excellently spiced and tasty and comes with an interesting collection of salad leaves. The big surprise is the catch of the day, which on one visit consisted of spanking fresh fillets of sole steamed in lettuce with a pungently ginger cream sauce, better-than-average vegetables and waxy potatoes. The view from above is compelling.

Restaurant information

Getting there: Underground – Buchanan Street
Landmark:
Open: Seven days; Mon–Fri 11a.m.–midnight, Sat 11.00a.m.–11.45p.m., Sun 7.00–11.00p.m.
Price per head (average): £4.50 (lunch) £10.00 (dinner); American Express, Access and Visa cards accepted.
Facilities: Smoking in part.
Vegetarian food available

JUNKANOO ♟
111 Hope Street   041-248 7102

The entrance to this tapas bar on the relentless traffic-dominated junction at the side of Central station is somehow less than appealing. The premises themselves are long, narrow and tapering back from the door – an interior decorator's nightmare. The management has evidently decided to cast tourist Spain aside for a dark, Hispanic, bodega-like effect which conjures impoverished Latin America, with fashionably functional grey plaster walls, modernistic murals, the odd Latin America Solidarity poster, fun chairs (if you only intend to sit on them for a short while) and rows of chilli peppers threaded up and displayed on the wall. There are about thirty different tapas from which to choose, if you include the changing daily specials (such as chargrilled sardines) all offered at affordable prices which encourage experimentation and a sense of adventure. There's a lot of garlic going about and generous amounts of virgin olive oil so you can't go too far wrong. Basics include Serrano ham, chorizo sausage, Manchego cheese, olives, decent tortilla Espanola, squid, octopus and mixed salad. Then there's well spiced marinated aubergine (hard to make anything of the tasteless Dutch variety that dominates Scottish markets but this is a good try), crisp fried toasts with uncommercial mayonnaise, topped with silvery boquerones, freshly cooked chicken with garlic in unctuous olive-oil juices, sauteed peppers (too plainly done to be interesting) and much more. To wash all this down, there is an discerning selection of dry sherries served chilled, wines and Aqua Libra, freshly squeezed orange juice by the glass, or energising espresso coffee. Ideal for flexible eating, low prices, amiable service.

Restaurant information

Getting there: Underground – St Enoch
Landmark: Central Station
Open: Mon–Sat; 12 noon till late
Price per head (average): £1.00–£5.95; American Express cards accepted.
Facilities: Wheelchair access, no disabled toilet; children welcome; smoking throughout.
Vegetarian food available

KENSINGTON'S
164 Darnley Street   041-424 3662

You walk through Kensington's drab exterior into a plush, velvety-red sub-Victorian decor with a display of tartan and whisky as the centrepiece. The food, in common with the decor, is highly conservative, on first view positively anachronistic (Steak Diane, Stilton and port 'Conrad Hilton', flambé sweets and so on). This is a popular restaurant which will appeal to those who want to feel pampered, who like to select from conventional, unchallenging Franco-British food and who do not expect to pay too much for it. Within the limitations of these structural constraints, Kensington's is a decent performer, serving good quality ingredients, reasonably cooked and offering excellent rapport qualité prix. Select starters include flavoursome home-made soups such as chicken and avocado, or ripe fresh pear with crisp salad and tarragon flavoured crème fraiche. Main courses include gargantuan portions of tender beef, awash with a gravy-like juice and overcooked (regulars may like it this way), or a slight breast of Gressingham duck in an altogether superior orange sauce – tart and fresh, not bulked out with sugar or cornflour. Vegetables come on the side, rather too many and too soft, but pepped up by the addition of garlic butter. The management displays an inability to spell its selection of Scottish farmhouse cheeses accurately, and a vagueness about its geographical location (Dunsyre Blue from Ayrshire?), but much more to the point, succeeds in presenting a judicious range in absolutely perfect condition. The cheese plate comes with an unctuous, ripe Bonchester wedge, melting Dunsyre blue, that sweet ewe's cheese Craigrossie , a charcoal-dusted and goaty Madoch, plus a young, but crumbly and uncommercial Cheddar. Desserts show more evidence of good buying. The chocolate mousse is rich and fudgy, testimony to good bitter chocolate, there are crisp filo baskets, and fresh, again not oversweet, fruit coulis. Staff are strong on asking you if everything is all right, but fairly uninformed about the nature or content of dishes. The set lunch is an outstanding bargain.

Restaurant information

Getting there: Train – Pollokshields
Landmark: Tramway Theatre
Open: Mon–Sat; Mon–Fri 12 noon–2.30p.m.; Mon–Sat 6.30–10.30p.m.
Price per head (average): £8.95 (lunch) £20.00 (dinner); all major credit cards accepted.
Facilities: Wheelchair access, no disabled toilet; children welcome; smoking throughout.
Vegetarian food available

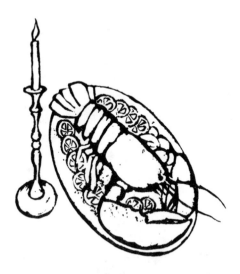

LA PARMIGIANA ░░░
447 Great Western Road   041-334 0686

As Tinelli's is to Edinburgh, so La Parmigiana is to Glasgow – unaffected and authentic Italian food which makes a break with the British trattoria tradition. This is cooking which starts off with the right ingredients and then allows them to speak for themselves. The menu is full of stimulating choices, vitello tonnato (the classic veal in a tuna and anchovy sauce), bollito misto (chicken, veal and zampone poached with vegetables and served with salsa verde), a proper carpaccio of excellent beef with lemon, olive oil and parmesan, or Livornese fish stew. Prime Scottish ingredients get the Italian treatment, such as monkfish roasted with pancetta (Italian bacon). This kitchen obviously feels no need to show off, so it will provide you with an antipasto of good Parma ham, fresh mozzarella, marinated aubergine, and chopped anchovies and parsley on toast with only olive oil as embellishment. Chargrilled quail come pink and juicy, deliciously seared with lemon juice in place of the ostentatious sauces which might envelop them elsewhere. There are good pastas, and unusual ones – paparadelle, orecciette – with home-made pesto, porcini in tomato sauce, Italian salciccia and more. Vegetables are conventional but properly cooked and fresh, salads suitably Italianate – good raddichio and so on. Lemony pine kernel tart with a rich custard layer looks dry but tastes moist and home-baked or there is a version of crème brûlée flavoured with strega in place of the bought-in ice-cream desserts that are so ubiquitous in Italian ristorante. The setting for this honest food is pleasant, airy and restrained if one ignores the ornamental tile roofs and windows which combined with upfront oompa music give a mock Alpine effect. Service is impeccable – relaxed, efficient – and there is some classy and expensive Italian wine to be drunk.

Restaurant information

Getting there: Underground – Kelvinbridge
Landmark: Kelvinbridge
Open: Mon–Sat; 12 noon–2.30p.m. and 6.00–11.00p.m.
Price per head (average): £5.20 (lunch) £15.00 (dinner); all major credit cards accepted.
Facilities: Wheelchair access, no disabled toilet; children welcome; smoking throughout.
Vegetarian food available

LA PATISSERIE FRANÇOISE 🍴
138a Byres Road   041-334 1882

Walking past, you could be forgiven for thinking that you were in France. Here's a windowful of good looking tarts, fondant coated choux confections and mille feuilles. Inside, the golden espresso machine glints, the revolving display cabinet with bonbons moves silently around and people come to feel continental or while away a minute or two. The cakes are no worse than many you might get in la belle France, though they could be better. Signs of pandering to Scottish palates show in the commercial milk shakes which share a shelf with good French siropes. Scottish snacks at lunch include chicken soup or vegetable lasagne and offer less inspiration. But the coffee will send caffeine addicts out feeling regenerated.

Restaurant information

Getting there: Underground – Hillhead
Landmark: Glasgow University
Open: Mon–Sat; 9.30a.m.–6.30p.m.
Price per head (average): £4.00; **no credit cards accepted**
Facilities: Children welcome; smoking throughout.
Vegetarian food available
Other services: Carry-out.

L'ARIOSTA ♟♟
92–94 Mitchell Street   041-221 0971

A glance through L'Ariosta's menu will provoke a sense of *déjà vu*
in some, boredom in others, or a feeling of security in those who
like a familiar range of Italian or international dishes. Much of the
menu is predictable – prosciutto with melon, steak, veal alla
Milanese, chicken Kiev, Zabaglione, crepes Suzette and so on. Yet
this restaurant is streets ahead of others which might appear at
first quite similar, because L'Ariosta is distinguished by offering a
polished performance from start to finish. Professionalism shows
in both the cooking and in the service, which if you like it attentive,
is as near to perfection as you'll get. The restaurant is large, with
various discreet elements, a bar, and a dance floor. (Dinner dances
are *de rigueur* here.) Mock balconies overhang the dance floor and
there are decorative Tyrolean-looking roofs. If all this sounds like
overkill, be reassured that the prevailing style is cool and
substantial, relying on natural materials such as good ceramic
tiles, exposed stone and brick for its effect. Two dishes sum up the
classy performance that this kitchen can give. First, a generous
fillet of pearly, moist turbot topped with thin slices of rindless
lemon, topped in turn with buttery croutons served in buttery
lemon juices. Next, fork-tender rings of patently fresh, not frozen,
squid in a fishy tomato sauce spiked with capers. Simple vegetables, waxy steamed potatoes, and crisp, if old-fashioned, salads
accompany. Institutions like steak are faultlessly executed, and
garnished without fussing and tarting up. Busy at lunch with
business people who can be assured of good service and reliable
food that remains immune from passing fashion; in the evening,
popular with those seeking good cooking, comfort and a taste of
romance.

Restaurant information

Getting there: Underground – St Enoch
Landmark: Central station
Open: Mon–Sat; 11.00a.m.–2.30p.m. and 5.00p.m.–11.00p.m.
Price per head (average): £10.00 (lunch) £18.00 (dinner); all major
credit cards accepted.
Facilities: Children welcome; smoking throughout.
Vegetarian food available

LOON FUNG ♫
417 Sauchiehall Street   041-332 1477

Popular Glasgow Cantonese, well-loved for its impressive array of Chinese snacks (dim sum). You take your pick from the twenty or so appetisers (all under £2) and order more when and if you need them. The steamed glutinous rice in lotus leaves is compelling, a veritable treasure trove of kitchen scraps spanning everything from duck to spicy sausage, with a moreish crispy crust. Deep-fried won ton encasing a plump prawn are ably executed, with no trace of the old oil flavours which often destroy such dishes elsewhere. A light, almost Japanese Tempura-style batter graces the squid, unfortunately chewy enough to suggest that it has been frozen. Beef dumplings steamed with onions are gelatinous in texture, with an intoxicating aroma of fresh ginger. There is a selection of steamed rice rolls with various fillings – the roast pork version (char sui) is excellent. There are signs of pandering to the untutored palates of Scottish diners. It is hard to believe that the Chinese themselves would enjoy the lurid red sweet and sour concoction which is served as a dipping sauce, in place of a good home-made dipping sauce or even commercial hoisin sauce. Main courses are generous and well-done, offering the usual range of Cantonese dishes. There are vegetarian set meals. The setting is spacious, relaxed and very efficient, (you could eat here on your own without feeling out of place though sheer portion size might defeat you). Staff are friendly and fast, and can take you through your meal at a cracking pace, if this is what you want. Children are treated like little emperors. Nice touches like an unsolicited plate of clementines to finish your meal send customers away happy. Very affordable.

Restaurant information

Getting there: Underground – St George's Cross/Cowcaddens
Open: Seven days; 12noon–11.30p.m.
Price per head (average): £6.00 (lunch) £13.00 (dinner); American Express, Access and Visa cards accepted.
Facilities: Children welcome; smoking throughout.
Vegetarian food available

MAI THAI 🍴
415 Sauchiehall Street   041-332 4996

Persevere beyond the unconvincing stairway entrance. Mai Thai offers a tantalising glimpse into the spirit of Thai cuisine, full of contrasting sensations – hot, sweet, sour, salty – and the intriguing flavours of galangal, lemon grass, shrimp paste and much more. For starters, there are miniature seaweed-wrapped prawn and pork roulades served with a soy dipping sauce, or a piquant salad of shredded carrots, chilli, sun-cured shrimps and grilled peanuts. A careful hand with deep-frying shows through in squid fried in the lightest of batters or fritters with a spicy peanut and vegetable sauce. Tiny spring rolls with a plum sauce prove more tempting than standard, heavyweight Chinese versions. Main courses are presented in the traditional Thai way – several dishes served simultaneously. These may include variously yam neua, thin marinated strips of grilled beef with a chilli and lemon sauce over glass noodles, and tom bohtaak, a spicy seafood soup of crab claws, squid and prawns vividly flavoured with lemon grass. Stir-fried noodles with broccoli, or an omelette of minced pork, offer blander contrasts to a forceful chicken and aubergine curry flavoured with coconut and other chilli-laden rice dishes. This is generally not a menu for the fainthearted. Chilli and ginger elbow subtler spices into second place. Overall, educational and fun, though the authentic vibrant freshness of tropical fruits and vegetables is understandably lacking.

Restaurant information

Getting there: Train – Charing Cross; Bus – 57/44/11/59
Landmark: Charing Cross
Open: Mon–Sat; 12 noon–3.00p.m. and 6.30–11.00p.m.
Price per head (average): £5.50 (lunch) £12.50 (dinner); all major credit cards accepted.
Facilities: Children welcome; smoking throughout.
Vegetarian food available.
Other services: Carry out

MATA HARI 🎭🎭
17 West Princes Sreet   041-332 9789

In amongst the tattoo parlours and moneylenders in the colourful terrain behind the Tron Theatre, you'll find this postage-stamp-sized non-smoking Malaysian restaurant with its proud boast 'We never compromise on quality and authenticity'. It's run by a idiosyncratic, but extremely likeable Scot whose talented Malaysian wife makes stall or hawker food and the resulting tastes leave other Scottish 'Malaysian' restaurants in the shade. You can pick out individual flavours like the lemon grass which flavours rump steak. The mixed Penang noodles served in a brimming bowl make a brilliant one-course lunch:rice and egg noodles, fish balls, beansprouts, chicken and much more in a 3-D coconut flavoured sauce. Various combinations of fish, shellfish and vegetables come in a mild and fruity sweet and sour sauce with a hint of chilli, which carefully eschews the corrosive qualities so often encountered in this kind of sauce.The quirkiness of the proprietor is part of its charm, as is the decor, reminiscent of a liberal kindergarten art class. They have no licence so you take your own wine or beer.
* Stop press: just moved to new and larger premises as we go to press. This review relates to the old venue in Parnie Street.

Restaurant information

Open: Mon–Sat; Mon 6–11.00p.m.; Tues–Thurs 12 noon–2.00p.m. and 6–11.00p.m.; Fri–Sat 12 noon–2.00p.m. and 6–11.30p.m.
Price per head (average): £4.50 (lunch) £10.00 (dinner); Access and Visa cards accepted.
Vegetarian food available.

ONE DEVONSHIRE GARDENS 🍴🍴
1 Devonshire Gardens 041-339 2001

This is a lavish Victorian Glasgow villa which has been deftly refurbished under the inspired judgment of Ken McCulluch to make a small hotel and restaurant. There is nothing reverential or conformist in its approach, but the style (dark, strong, comfortable and unfussy) somehow feels in keeping with the building's original character. The food, in common with the decor, observes the traditional structures, but plays around within them a bit. Results are capable, in the modern vein, offering little in the way of originality. Choices are sensibly limited and there's plenty of evidence that the kitchen takes prime materials as its starting point. Starters range over warm salads (chicken liver and almonds), raw chopped beef fillet with capers, a light pastry case filled with succulent and sensitively cooked mussels in a surprisingly successful brie sauce, or a delightfully textured fresh terrine of salmon, sole and scallops. For main courses, some simple, classical dishes are excellently well-accomplished – witness a moist breast of chicken stuffed with a strong tarragon mousseline. Modern renditions, such as marinated beef fillet with wasabi and pickled ginger, make an appearance. A mille feuille of sea-trout in season, turns out to be more of a roulade, but every bit as delicious in any event. Vegetarians are ignored (as far as the menu goes anyway) and the prominence of raw beef and beef offal may limit the choice for green-minded diners. For dessert there's an immaculate mango and passion fruit souffle, brown bread and coconut ice-cream, an airy toasted caramel mousse and more in that style. Service is polished, observant and efficient, but unstuffy in a refreshingly Glasgow style.

Restaurant information

Getting there: Underground – Hyndland; Bus – 20/59/66/51/44/11
Open: Seven days; 12 noon–2.00p.m. and 7.00–11.00p.m.
Price per head (average): £17.50 (lunch) £27.50 (dinner); American Express, Diners, Visa and Access cards accepted.
Facilities: Children welcome; smoking throughout.
Vegetarian food available by prior arrangement

THE ORIENT ♟
St Enoch Centre, Argyle Street

The giant decorative wok and chopsticks which sits like an insignia over the Orient is great fun and the food which emerges from the sizzling kitchen behind is good, mainstream Chinese, as you might expect from the proprietors of Glasgow's Peking Inn. The Orient is clean, fast and generous in quantity with a variety of Cantonese and Pekinese main courses (and ersatz dishes like chicken with mushroom, tactfully referred to as 'old favourites') served with fresh fried rice. The crispy shredded Peking beef, stiff with sesame seeds, has a robust chilli-hot flavour with pungent strands of root ginger and sweet red pepper lemon chicken is lightly interpreted and free of food colourings. All the food is piping hot. By far the best of the fast food options on offer to dizzy skaters or dazed shoppers in the St Enoch Centre.

Restaurant information

Getting there: Underground – Argyle Street & St Enoch Centre
Landmark: St Enoch Centre
Open: Mon–Sat; Mon–Wed 9.00a.m. 6.00p.m., Thurs 9.00a.m.–8.00p.m., Fri–Sat 9.00a.m.–6.00p.m.
Price per head (average): £3.60; no credit cards accepted.
Facilities: Wheelchair access; disabled toilet; children welcome; smoking in part.
Vegetarian food available
Other services: Carry-out.

PEKING INN 🍴
191 Hope Street   041-332 8971/7120

Waves of hungry office workers descend on the Peking Inn at lunch-time like first year schoolboys queueing for seconds. This is formula Chinese eating, tasty and flavoursome, designed to suit the Scottish palate. Not that this kitchen is incapable of more authentic cooking but more that its Scottish customers might not thank it for this. But with a discerning selection on the full evening menu, there are good things to be had, indeed certain dishes are too good to miss. There are for example, magnificent 'potsticker' style dumplings (described only as fresh meat dumpling), where chewy dumpling wrappers are filled with tender pork, first steamed and then fried – perfect of their kind. Fresh sole comes cooked to good effect in a light batter, with a deep and natural flavoured sauce full of root ginger, mushrooms and Chinese leaves. Rich braised duck in the Szechuan style is chilli-spicy and unctuous, complemented by the inclusion of fresh green leek.

Vegetarians get better treatment than in many Chinese restaurants. They can choose from various renditions of beancurd, the Buddha dish (an all-in-one vegetable dish) or a crispy vegetable roll with capital sauce – crunchy baby corn, bamboo shoot, beansprouts and wood ear mushroom inside crisp pastry like a sort of giant spring roll. The vibrantly red capital sauce though, is a blockbuster, which delicate palates may find overpowering. Basics, like spring rolls and fried rice get a lighter-than-average touch. The decor inclines to a positive degree of comfort and ostentation with plush seats, festoon blinds and linen tablecloths. Staff, when not concentrating on threading their way through gaps in tables with food-laden trays, are friendly enough.

Restaurant information

Getting there: Underground – Buchanan Street
Landmark: Odeon theatre
Open: Mon–Sat; 12 noon–11.30p.m.
Price per head (average): £5.00 (lunch) £15.00 (dinner); American Express, Diners, Visa and Access cards accepted
Facilities: Wheelchair access, no disabled toilet; children welcome; smoking throughout.
Vegetarian food available
Other services: Carry-out service

PENGUIN CAFE 🐧🐧

Rooftop Princes Square, 46 Buchanan Street   041-221 0303

A triumphant celebration of black and white and Thirties style, the Penguin Cafe makes a stylish and cosmopolitan setting for an eclectic menu, which spans several continents but comes down firmly in the camp of New York-style modern food. Bar snacks include superior renditions of chilli con carne and club sandwiches, deep-fried potato skins and stuffed pitta pockets. Less casual food, served in the calmer dining area, include a proper chopped steak burger, blackened swordfish steak, salmon wrapped in filo or grilled with a basil pesto and plenty of vegetarian choices from lasagnes to stir fry. Salads are exciting, such as curly endive with bacon, stilton and croutons topped with a lightly poached egg. The kitchen is not short of good ingredients – virgin olive oil, balsamic vinegar and fresh herbs are very much in evidence. Sticky toffee pudding is hard to ignore.

Restaurant information

Getting there: Underground – Buchanan Street
Landmark: Princes Square
Open: Mon–Sat; Mon–Thurs 11.00a.m.–11.00p.m., Fri–Sat 11.00a.m.–midnight.
Price per head (average): £5.00–10.00; American Express, Visa, Access, Diners and Mastercard cards accepted.
Facilities: Wheelchair access, no disabled toilet; children welcome; smoking throughout.
Vegetarian food available

PJ'S PASTARIA

Maryfield House, Ruthven Lane   041-339 0932

Very basic cheap and cheerful food which makes for easy and accessible eating for all the family. There are all the standard pastas and sauces like Milanese with cheese, ham and mushrooms and stalwart basics like lasagne. PJ'S also specialises in home-made pasta sauces with a difference like chicken curry and beef with Guinness. There are monumental ice-cream sundaes, beer by the jug and special offers to be had by the vigilant, such as the happy hour (two actually) between 5.00 p.m. and 7.00 p.m. on quieter days when all pasta dishes are half price. Children get their own menu. PJ's also have an outlet in the food court in Princes Square.

Restaurant information

Getting there: Underground – Hillhead
Landmark: Glasgow University
Open: Seven days; Mon–Fri 12 noon –2.30p.m. and 5.00p.m.–midnight, Sat–Sun 12 noon–midnight.
Price per head (average): £3.00-£4.00 (lunch) £8.00-£10.00 (dinner); half price pasta Sun–Thurs 5.00–7.00p.m.; Visa and Access cards accepted.
Facilities: Wheelchair access, no disabled toilet; children welcome; smoking in part only.
Vegetarian food available
Other services: Carry-out; Children's menu available; 'al fresco' eating on the patio, weather permitting.

RAJDOOT ♟
11–13 Hyndland Street   041-334 0084

This popular neighbourhood restaurant produces worthwhile, if not outstanding Indian food which avoids the worst pitfalls of the curry house tradition. It is served amidst aspiring decor – pink and green walls the colour of Indian confectionery, chandeliers and colonial style fans. Frills apart, the menu is not over-long, fairly standard but decently executed. Pakora demonstrate a lighter-than-average touch, not weighed down by an excess of gram flour, but moist and interestingly flavoured with whole fennel seed and green pepper. These are served with a robustly chilli-flavoured lentil sauce. Samosas are of generous dimensions, encased in a crisp crust and unusually stuffed with diced rather than minced lamb. The essentials are well done. There are capable breads (well-fired nans and crunchy pooris), and rice is discreetly pale yellow with a full basmati scent. There is some variety to the curries. Vegetables are delicately cubed, dry and briefly tossed in spices, dhall is soupy and thick, chicken in a rich gravy flavoured with cinnamon. The house kulfi is soft and toothsome with a fresh mango flavour. Featherweight gulab jamon come soaked in restrained sugary syrup. Waiters in military outfits show, on occasion, Basil Fawlty-ish tendencies which assertive diners will have little difficulty ignoring.

Restaurant information

Getting there: Underground – Kelvinhall; Bus – 62/64/9/12/5/5A
Landmark: Glasgow Art Gallery and Musuem
Open: Seven days; Mon–Fri; 12 noon–2.00p.m. and 5.00p.m.–midnight; Sat 12 noon–midnight; Sun 5.00p.m.–midnight.
Price per head (average): £4.50 (lunch) £9.50 (dinner); Visa, Access, Diners and American Express cards accpeted.
Facilities: Children welcome; smoking in part.
Vegetarian food available
Other services: Home delivery and carry-out

RESTAURANT OCTOBER ♙♙
128 Drymen Road, Bearsden   041-942 7272

Ferrier Richardson is a serious Scottish chef in the modern vein. His restaurant, situated in this douce and well-heeled suburb, is giving more established city restaurants some stiff competition. This is a restaurant that has been thoroughly interior-decorated. The style is East Coast American, lots of money but laid back about it. Cool, aesthetic, simple mirrors, twinkling lights and caressingly comfortable seating. Contemporary Glasgow rock, well-chosen, plays in suitably muted tones. Staff are articulate and egalitarian. All this makes a change from the second grade country house hotel approach to which so many ambitious Scottish establishments aspire. The menu will appear familiar to those who dine out at this level frequently. Mushroom feuilletes, carrot and coriander soup, steak, calf's liver with parsley and lemon butter, brandy snap baskets, fruit sorbets with complementary fruit coulis, crème brûlée and so on. Saucing is assertive, on occasion aggressive, pastry a strong point. Overall, there's evidence of good taste. Although this kitchen will top a perfectly wonderful fish soup with an unnecessary, if delicious herb souffle, it knows not to stick a cape gooseberry on to the turbot or a slice of star fruit over the venison. Vegetables get the standard side dish treatment, plain and butter coated – wholly boring. Vegetarians get a couple of starter choices followed by one main course possibility. Desserts are a strong point, deeply vanilla-flavoured ice-cream, decent sorbets, hot Grand Marnier souffles, shortbread walnut and caramel tarts. In total, a thoroughly pleasant environment serving classy food at reasonable prices – the set lunch menu is incredibly cheap. Wines, however, are not particularly special and border on pricey.

Restaurant information

Getting there: Train – Bearsden or Hillfoot; Bus – 18/26
Landmark: Bearsden Cross
Open: Mon–Sat; 12 noon–2.00p.m. and 7.00–10.00p.m. Sunday lunch only
Price per head (average): £10.50 (lunch) £25.00 (dinner); Visa and Access cards accepted.
Facilities: Wheelchair access and disabled toilet; children welcome; smoking permitted but with consideration for fellow diners.
Vegetarian food available

RISTORANTE CAPRESE ♟
217 Buchanan Street   041-332 3070

The surrounding environs and entrance which lead to this much-loved Italian restaurant are deeply unlovely. There is absolutely nothing to draw the passing visitor inside. None of this matters to the Caprese management who can count on word of mouth and repeat custom to pack out the place. Caprese enthusiasts rarely begin their description by talking about the food. First and foremost, the regulars love the atmosphere. More than likely their photos will be on the wall, or at the very least they can expect to be fussed over by Constanzo and Ernesto whose warmth and informality has put this establishment on the map. Not that the food is wanting – the standard of presentation is high with the correct emphasis on flavour over presentation – but it offers little in the way of originality and poses no new challenges. Among the more exciting starters is a creamy egg Florentine with tender fresh spinach or rustic bean and pasta soup, served with a generous splash of olive oil. In amongst the standard bill of fare (steak Diane, routine pastas and so on) you will find fritto misto, saltinbocca – veal with parma ham and sage – and tender baby squid in a tomato and herb sauce, all deliciously rendered. Limited desserts – crema caramella, peach melba, ice-cream, zabaglione – but opulent alcoholic, creamy coffees for those who like that sort of thing.

Restaurant information

Getting there: Underground – Buchanan Street
Landmark: New Concert Hall.
Open: Mon–Sat; 12 noon–2.30p.m. and 5.30–11.00p.m.
Price per head (average): £6.00 (lunch) £13.00 (dinner); American Express, Diner, Access and Visa cards accepted.
Facilities: Smoking throughout.
Vegetarian food available

ROGANO 🍳🍳
11 Exchange Square   041-248 4055

A trip to the Rogano feels a bit like a visit to the theatre or to the set of a Fred Astaire film. Your coat is taken at the door and you are ushered inside to goggle at the sights. So splendid and sumptuous is the famed Thirties decor of the Rogano, (built and furnished in the same style as the Queen Mary and practically in original condition), that style enthusiasts might be prepared to pay for this alone. There's no doubt that the Rogano is a revered Glasgow institution, witnessed by its dynamic clientele which includes many a well-known face. Fortunately, the cooking is generally good, if patchy, with an emphasis on traditional fish favourites like Dover sole, salmon and lobster, or the reliable Rogano fish soup – rich and velvety, accompanied by toast generously spread with rouille. But there are more vogueish renditions like turbot wrapped in cabbage with a watercress sauce or large prawns flavoured with root ginger. Ingredients are fresh and well-selected. Desserts a bit disappointing. Cafe Rogano down in the basement serves more affordable high standard brasserie food. There's a generous seafood fried rice spilling over with plump crustaceans or more unusual combinations like chicken coated with blue poppy seeds served with a mild, aromatic cumin sauce. American-style salads like bacon with parmesan croutons and garlic dressing come sensibly, either as a side dish or scaled up as a main course. Nostalgia music creates a background for the relaxed buzz. The ambience is intimate and stylish, service of the perceptive variety. You pay through the nose for coffee, but it does thereafter arrive in plentiful supply.

Restaurant information

Getting there: Underground – Buchanan Street
Landmark: Stirling Library
Open: Restaurant Mon–Sat; 12 noon–2.30p.m. and 6.00–10.30p.m.; Cafe Mon–Thurs 12 noon–11.00p.m. Fri–Sat 12 noon–midnight.
Price per head (average): Restaurant £30.00–£35.00, Cafe £12.00–£15.00; Access, Visa, Diners and American Express cards accepted.
Facilities: Wheelchair access, no disabled toilet; children welcome; smoking throughout.
Vegetarian food available

SANNINO 🍴🍴

61 Bath Street   041-332 8025 and 81 Elmbank Street 041-332 3565

Tough luck for those who believe that corporate ownership is the death knell for decent food. Both Sanninos are owned by Stakis Leisure and the food is unarguably good. Best to know this in advance because despite the menu's proud boast that 'authenticity is the key word . . . the Sannino experience is about genuine Neapolitan recipes prepared in modern kitchens . . . no deep freezers and microwaves', the plush Seventies pub style decor might cause one to be suspicious. The decor is glitzy, opulent, undeniably comfortable and the background music subliminal Carpenters. The menu looks like a million others and craves your indulgence for the twenty to twenty-five minute wait that serious pasta and pizza takes. In reality it emerges faster than that. Pastas (there are twelve, five of which are vegetarian) go beyond safe acceptable limits, with rich sauces and delicious flavouring. Linguine alle zucchinii is almost unctuous, with a base flavour of good pesto, nicely reduced with cream and wafer-thin courgettes to relieve the texture. The pizzas are a triumph, light, crisp on both sides with compulsively flaky edges, topped with grade one produce – good mozzarella, parma ham, smoked salmon, Milano salami or simple anchovies or black olives. The pizzas are not cheap – the management recommends one between two – but this is using Bunteresque measurements. The wines are 100 per cent prosaic but not particularly expensive by most standards. The staff behave as if they have been on a 'How to be nice to the customers course,' which results in happy, bow-tied, garrulous service, prompt attention and believe it or not, the opportunity to grind your own black pepper and help yourself to parmesan.

Restaurant information

Open: Seven days; 12 noon–midnight
Price per head (average): £5.00 (lunch) £7.00 (dinner); Access, Visa, American Express, Style, Diners and Switch cards accepted.
Facilities: Wheelchair access; disabled toilet; children welcome; smoking throughout.
Vegetarian food available
Other services: Carry-out

THE TRIANGLE 🍴🍴🍴
37 Queen Street   041-221 8758

If there is one eating place that has done something to shake up Glaswegian, indeed Scottish, notions about food, it is the Triangle. It fits neither of the popular urban styles of dining out: the choice between good food in formal and often stuffy settings or a trendy, stylish environment serving casual bistro food. The Triangle inhabits vast and airy premises and the decor is inspired – part Manhattan loft, part Conran. Space is fluid. The bar runs into the brasserie and from there runs into the dining-room. The food is as flexible as the space. One of the Triangle's big assets is a range of dishes around £4 which you can have as starter or light main course. These include a generous warm salad of scallops and bacon dressed with a nut oil vinaigrette, or a crispy home-made confit of duck served with a tart red onion 'marmalade'. The meat or fish and two veg formula is refreshingly replaced with dishes which are complete in themselves, like skate with beurre noisette and capers or chicken steamed with coriander and ginger, served in a rush basket. Top quality ingredients shine through. Desserts are heavenly, witness a sumptuous dark, white and milk chocolate terrine or a rich eggy tart with sound crème anglaise. There's a serious artisan cheese board to toy with. The wine list is passionate, quirky and unusually varied and a cruover machine keeps wine by the glass in good nick.

Restaurant information

Getting there: Train – Central & Queen Street Stations; Underground – Buchanan Street & St Enoch Centre;
Landmark: Above Tam Sheperd's Trick Shop
Open: Mon–Sat; 12 noon–3.00p.m. and 7.00–10.30p.m.
Price per head (average): £10.00 (lunch) £20.00 (dinner); all major credit cards accepted.
Facilities: Children over 14 years old welcome in the restaurant; smoking throughout.
Vegetarian food available

TWO FAT LADIES ♨
88 Dumbarton Road   041-339 1944

Exterior signs suggest an interest in cooking rather than surroundings. Once inside, the decor belies that, cool and minimalist in a fashionable way. The menu is written on artistically etched glass and attached to the wall. In case the spelling mistakes confuse you, the menu (heavy on fish), is also verbally proposed with embellishments – 'Oysters fresh today from the Isle of . . .' and so on. Wines, (there are only a handful, so you may prefer to bring your own) receive vaguer treatment. 'Cotes du Rhone. I think it's French'. If you don't mind being on the receiving end of good ideas which could sometimes do with more polishing then this is a fun place to dine. Grilled herring with Japanese horseradish (wasabi) and daikon radish tastes less interesting than it sounds. The fish soup is pleasant enough though it smells and tastes overwhelmingly of garlic rather than fish. Fish comes in gargantuan portions, sometimes in the case of a rich fish like tuna, rather self-defeating. Chargrilled aubergine wedges with a rustic home-made tomato sauce offer vegetarians respite from fish. Better-than-average vegetables, including nicely glazed slices of sweet potato. Desserts are mainstream *Good Housekeeping*: apple tart, meringue confections, chocolate mousse or roulade. How you feel about the prices will depend on how you feel about the cooking.

Restaurant information

Getting there: Underground – Kelvinhall
Landmark: City Art Gallery and Museums
Open: Tues–Sun; 7.00–10.30p.m. (last orders)
Price per head (average): £15.00; Visa, Access, Mastercard and Eurocard cards accepted.
Facilities: Wheelchair access, disabled toilet; children welcome; smoking throughout.
Vegetarian food available

UBIQUITOUS CHIP 🍺🍺
12 Ashton Lane   041-334 5007/7109

One of Glasgow's good food institutions, where you are guaranteed a reliably high standard of food. The Chip is not cheap, and part of the price has to be the atmosphere – tables nestle in a covered courtyard area among lush greenery with tropical plants and potted shrubs in abundance – plus the opportunity to play Who's Who with that day's clientele (BBC, academics and so on). First class Scottish ingredients are the order of the day: West coast seafood, excellent game and fine handmade cheeses like Lanark Blue. The food is basically modern in style but without the uncontrolled eclecticism of other followers of the genre. Pigeon comes with a wild mushroom sauce and a good red wine reduction, or fillets of turbot with a crunchy pine kernel and green peppercorn crust. Admirably executed old favourites like braised oxtail and silverside will appeal to traditionalists. The Chip exploits the Taste of Scotland theme without courting tweeness. Clapshot, oatmeal ice-cream and venison haggis make regular appearances. Dishes like vegetable and nut baskets with pear and watercress sauce show that vegetarians are taken seriously. The Chip's wine list is deservedly famous and ungreedily priced. Positively sinful therefore, not to take full advantage of it.

Restaurant information

Getting there: Underground – Hillhead
Landmark: Behind Hillhead Underground
Open: Seven days; Lunch Mon–Sat 12 noon–2.30p.m. Sun 12.30–4.00p.m.; Dinner Mon–Sat 5.30–11.00p.m., Sun 6.30–11.00p.m., Pub Food 11.00a.m.–11.00p.m.
Price per head (average): £18.00 (lunch) £20.00 (dinner); Access, Visa, Diners and American Express cards accepted
Facilities: Wheelchair access and disabled toilet; children welcome; smoking throughout.
Vegetarian food available.

WINTERGREEN CAFE 🏠
People's Palace, Glasgow Green   041-554 0195

If you are tiring of all the Glasgowing that's going on, then retreat to the magnificent People's Palace. It is a tremendous repository of Glasgow's real history and the dynamism of its management generates itself at all levels. The café is inside the Palace's beautiful Victorian conservatory, which in addition to a splendid array of plants and flowers, often has some other tasteful attractions inside, particularly for children. Metal furniture and parasols afford an opulent sense of leisure and the food is not exploitative in the way that many mass-catering tourist outfits are. This is vegetarian and wholefood, too worthwhile some might quibble. Cheese, onion and potato pie, vegetable pasties, wholemeal pizza and tomato and broccoli quiche provide options, plus a couple of daily salads – beansprout and waldorf for example. Baking (flapjack, rhubarb tart, caramel shortcake) is solid but good, with stout brown pastry and very little sugar. There are herbal teas in profusion, high quality fresh pressed apple juice and sensible mugs to be had. This is the sort of place where you can refresh a party of protesting, weary children (and adults for that matter) without paying a fortune for expensive junk. A lovely and deeply interesting place to spend some time. Relaxed staff with a helpful, egalitarian attitude.

Restaurant information

Getting there: Underground – St Enoch Centre; Bus – 18/61/64/14/62
Landmark: People's Palace
Open: Seven days; Mon–Wed; Fri–Sat 10.00am–4.15p.m. Thurs 10.00a.m.–9.15p.m., Sun 10.00a.m.–5.15p.m.
Price per head (average): £2.00–£2.50; No credit cards accepted.
Facilities: Wheelchair access, disabled toilets; children welcome; smoking throughout.
Vegetarian food available
Other services: Carry-out

SHOPPING IN EDINBURGH

VALVONA AND CROLLA, 19 Elm Row   (031) 556 6066
Italian foods and wines.
VICTOR HUGO, 26–27 Melville Terrace   667 1827
General delicatessen, farmhouse cheese.
NASTIUKC, 155 Bruntsfield Place   229 7054
General delicatessen, specialist fruit and vegetables.
REAL FOODS, 37 Broughton Street   557 1911
             8 Brougham Street   228 1201
Fresh and dry organic food, wholefoods.
GOURMET PASTA, 54–56 Morningside Road   447 4750
Fresh pasta, sauces and Italian specialities.
FLORENTIN, 25 Thistle Street   225 3103
French patisserie.
PAT'S CHUNG YING SUPERMARKET,
201 Leith Walk   554 0358
Chinese and south east Asian food.
GEORGE ARMSTRONG, 80 Raeburn Place   315 2033
Staple and more unusual fish, smoked salmon and oysters.
TSE'S FISH MARKET, 2 Warrender Park Road   662 4207
Staple and more unusual fish, shellfish.
GEORGE BOWER, 75 Raeburn Place   332 3469
Best Scottish meat and game.
CHARLES WILSON, 416 Morningside Road   452 9110
Organic beef, lamb and poultry.
PETER GREEN, 37 Warrender Park Road   229 5925
Outstanding independent wine merchant.
J. E. HOGG, 61 Cumberland Street   556 4025
Outstanding independent wine merchant.

SHOPPING IN GLASGOW

D'ARCY'S COMESTIBLES, Princes Square   (041) 221 5853
*Farmhouse cheese, delicatessen items
and wines.*

FAZZI BROTHERS, 67 Cambridge Street   332 0941
                 230–232 Clyde Street   221 9411
*Italian foods, home made sausages,
pastas and coffee.*

PECKHAM'S 100 Byres Road   357 1454
           43 Clarence Drive   357 2909
*General delicatessen items,
breads and wines.*

LIM'S CHUNG YING SUPERMARKET,
63 Cambridge Street   332 9399
Chinese and south-east Asian foods.

ROOTS AND FRUITS, 457 Great Western Road   334 3530
*Fresh organic, exotic and specialist
fruit and vegetables.*

GRASS ROOTS, 498 Great Western Road   334 1844
Wholefoods and organic food.

DASBROT, 51 Hyndland Road   334 8234
Rye breads.

BREADWINNER, 291 Byres Road   337 1642
Selection of breads.

ALAN BEVERIDGE, 1121 Pollokshaws Road   649 5067
              306 Byres Road   357 2766
Staple fish, more unusual fish and smoked fish.

JAMES MCKECHNIE, Shields Road Subway Station
Scotland Street   429 1609
*Smoked fish, staple and unusual fish,
prepared speciality fish, game.*

PAUL MURRAY, 117 Royston Road   552 2738
'Q' Guild butcher.

UBIQUITOUS CHIP WINE SHOP, 12 Ashton Lane   334 5007
Outstanding independent wine shop.